MILLION DOLLAR HABITS

10

SIMPLE STEPS TO GETTING EVERYTHING YOU WANT IN LIFE

ROBERT RINGER

SKYHORSE PUBLISHING

Skyhorse Publishing books may be purchased in bulk at special discounts for sales promotion, corporate gifts, fund-raising, or educational purposes. Special editions can also be created to specifications. For details, contact the Special Sales Department, Skyhorse Publishing, 307 West 36th Street, 11th Floor, New York, NY 10018 or info@skyhorsepublishing.com.

Skyhorse® and Skyhorse Publishing® are registered trademarks of Skyhorse Publishing, Inc. ®, a Delaware corporation.

www.skyhorsepublishing.com

10 9 8 7 6 5 4 3 2

Library of Congress Cataloging-in-Publication Data is available on file.

ISBN: 978-1-62636-398-4

Printed in China

TO MY FAMILY

CONTENTS

PREFACE

One of the most frequent questions directed at me in seminars is, "Knowing what you know today, would you change anything in your earlier books if you had the opportunity to do so?" What a question. Of course I would. It's like asking me if I'm dead or alive.

"We're all on our way to learning more," declared Don Shimoda, Richard Bach's messiah in *Illusions*. It would be difficult, if not impossible, for a person to learn and grow, yet remain static in his* thinking. While I haven't exactly become a card-carrying communist or self-immolating monk, I do continually strive to refine my basic philosophy.

An even tougher question with which someone recently confronted me was, "How would you define your occupation?" Interesting question, and one which, remarkably, had never before crossed my mind. After pondering for about twenty seconds, I answered, "I'm in the business of trying to make sense out of life and communicating my conclusions to others in the simplest possible manner." By at least one definition, I guess that

---

* Wherever the neuter is not used in this book, the masculine gender is employed for convenience purposes only. It has no other implications, implied or otherwise.

makes me a philosopher, because a philosopher is someone who thinks in an effort to make sense out of life.

What a great profession. Why work for a living when you can get away with thinking and typing all day? Of course, you risk going insane in the process, though I was fortunate enough to avoid such a fate until I moved to Los Angeles. (It was none other than Freud himself who warned people like me, "The moment one inquires about the sense or value of life, one is sick.") Still, in all, you know it's worth it when you check the classifieds and see what supermarkets are paying bag boys.

This book is a pretty accurate snapshot of where my thought evolution has taken me to date. To pick up my trail, just follow the path marked BUMPS, BRUISES, AND SCARS. If you keep your eyes and mind open and move briskly, you may even avoid a number of pitfalls along the way.

INTRODUCTION

The first major premise of this book is that success is not dependent upon one's being blessed with superior intelligence or special skills, nor does formal education, hard work, or luck play a major role in an individual's climb toward success. The world is saturated with intelligent, highly educated, extraordinarily skilled people who are perpetually frustrated because of their lack of success. Likewise, millions of others spend their lives working hard, long hours, only to die broke.

As to breaks, they float in and out of people's lives every day without being exploited or, in most cases, even noticed. You've undoubtedly known someone who has been the recipient of inordinately good luck, yet failed to achieve any significant degree of success. Heirs to large fortunes who are grossly unhappy, or who have lost their entire inheritances through reckless or irresponsible behavior, are classic examples of this sad phenomenon.

The second major premise of this book is that the difference between success and failure is not nearly as great as most people believe. Having personally experienced both major success and failure, I can state with confidence that the difference between the two is, in fact, quite slim.

The erroneous notion that there is a major difference between the actions of successful and unsuccessful people causes millions of individuals to cling to the mistaken belief that success is the result of being privy to some tenaciously guarded, mysterious secret. In the event you share this belief, I urge you to let go of it. I can absolutely assure you that there is no big secret to success.

Which leads me to the third and final major premise of this book: Success is matter of understanding and religiously practicing specific, simple habits that *always* lead to success. While this may not sound particularly glamorous at first blush, there are two realities that make it quite an exciting proposition: First, it works. Second, habits can be developed by anyone who is willing to put forth the necessary effort.

Remember, life is nothing more than the sum total of many successful years; a successful year is nothing more than the sum total of many successful months; a successful month is nothing more than the sum total of many successful weeks; and a successful week is nothing more than the sum total of many successful days. That's why practicing simple success habits day in and day out is the most certain way to come out on top over the long term.

Put in metaphorical terms, success is not a grand-slam home run. Rather, it's a matter of consistently hitting singles and doubles day in and day out. The individual who makes it to the top concentrates on staying at bat and avoiding the big mistake. Then, when that perfect pitch comes across the plate, he hits it out of the park.

The important principle to grasp is that if you don't keep hitting those singles and doubles every day, you may not have the opportunity to hit a home run when that perfect pitch finally arrives. In other words, you can't coast. You've got to do it every day.

The title *Million Dollar Habits* is a euphemism for habits that lead to positive results. Everyone gets results, regardless of the nature of his actions. A bank robber gets results. A person who refuses to work and goes on welfare gets results. An individual who is inconsiderate and rude gets results. But none of these people get positive results. So keep in mind that whenever I allude to *results* in this book, I'm talking about results that are in your *long-term* best interest.

One final note: Though the habits I discuss in this book are relatively simple, I don't mean to suggest that it takes no effort on your part to acquire and practice them. I never try to sell easy. I sell what I perceive to be truth.

CHAPTER 1

THE REALITY HABIT

Reality is the foundation for every other success habit, so in order for the ideas, strategies, and information that I discuss in this book to be of maximum benefit to you, it's crucial that you develop the Reality Habit. Except for an occasional accident of fate, positive results rarely find their way to people who harbor a faulty perception of reality. While many of the points in this chapter may seem obvious to you, that in itself can create a subtle barrier, because human beings have a tendency to ignore the obvious. Intellectually, we may agree with a point that's apparent, but when it comes time to take action, we often suppress our intellect and allow our emotions to guide us.

I use the word *emotions* because reality is an issue that people tend to get very emotional about. The problem is that reality is nothing more than truth, and as Baltasar Gracián, the insightful and pragmatic seventeenth-century Jesuit priest, cautioned, "Truth is abhorred by the masses." Instead, they try to make true that which they love—a self-delusive practice that virtually guarantees frustration and failure.

Unfortunately, most people live in an unreal world; i.e., they create a world in their own minds based on the way they would like it to be rather than the way it actually is. At one time or another, all of us seem to adopt the philosophy of humorist

Ashleigh Brilliant, who once remarked, "I have abandoned the search for truth, and am now looking for a good fantasy."

People often say things like, "But this is *my* reality. Reality is different for each person." Wrong. Reality is precisely the same for everyone. There is only one reality. What differs is each person's *perception* of reality. By *perception*, I am referring to the ability to correctly interpret the events that surround you, to be able to grasp the difference between what is real and what is unreal, between fact and fiction, between what works and what doesn't work. A faulty perception of reality is almost always destructive and sometimes fatal.

It's absolutely essential that a person intellectually and emotionally understands that reality isn't the way he wishes things to be or the way they appear to be, but the way they actually are. The person who is not able to make this distinction finds it virtually impossible to make decisions that lead to positive results.

Principles

As used in this chapter, a principle is synonymous with a law of nature, as opposed to a law of man. Most man-made laws are nothing more than legalized aggression against the sovereignty of peaceful individuals and rarely bear any relationship to Natural Law, reality, or morality. A man-made principle, such as Parkinson's Law, is not a true principle in the sense of being an immutable law. It is simply an observation of a human tendency. In the case of Parkinson's Law, it's merely our firsthand observations that lead us to concur that expenses tend to increase as income rises.

The most significant quality of a true principle of nature is that it can neither be created nor altered. The problem arises when people refuse to accept the reality that principles can only be discovered and insist on believing they can create their own.

Take the principle of gravity, for example. Isaac Newton didn't wake up one morning and decide to create a principle whereby if he dropped an apple from a tree twenty times, it would fall to the ground nineteen times and go up once. Ridiculous, of course. Instead, through experimentation, he *discovered* that if you drop an apple from a tree twenty times, it will fall to the ground twenty times. What he did was discover the principle, or law, of gravity.

A principle, then, is the essence of reality. It is what it is, and it's up to us to discover it. To try to create our own reality is both futile and destructive. You certainly have the right to go on believing whatever you wish to believe, but reality isn't discriminatory. It will mete out negative consequences just as harshly to the well-meaning, ignorant individual as to the malevolent, stubborn person. Not once has reality excused anyone for good motives, so consistency is essential when it comes to a proper perception of reality.

The Foundational Principle of Success

There are an infinite number of natural laws to be discovered, but, fortunately, you don't need a detailed understanding of every one of them to achieve even the most grandiose of goals. However, there is one law with which you must be totally familiar and that you must unfailingly use as a guide in all your dealings. The law I'm referring to is the ultimate, immutable law of nature, the foundation of reality itself: Actions Have Consequences.

If I push you (an action), something must happen; i.e., there must be a consequence. You may fall down, you may stumble, or, at the very least, you will feel pressure against your body. You may also get mad at me, walk away, or push me back. The point is that I cannot escape the reality that my action, no matter how small, will have consequences. Where I start to invite problems into my life is when I delude myself into believing that I can push you without there being any consequences. Every action that you and I have ever taken has, sooner or later, brought about a consequence.

In physics, we learn that for every action there is an equal and opposite reaction. The longer I live, however, the more convinced I am that in the daily process of living (as opposed to the science of physics), reactions tend to be *greater* than the actions that provoke them. Whenever we act improperly or dishonestly, the "punishment" seems to be way out of proportion to the "crime." My experience has been that I almost always end up paying for an irresponsible action over and over again, with each payment seeming to take the form of a balloon note carrying onerous, compounded interest.

The consequence may take a long time, and it may be indirect or subtle in nature, but there *is* always a consequence. Symbolically speaking, everything you do goes into your book of life. This doesn't necessarily hold a religious connotation, but I do firmly believe that universal forces are at work that pull us inexorably toward the deserving results of our actions. Kindness begets kindness; cruelty begets cruelty.

Where many people allow themselves to be misled is that the payback for their actions is not always immediate, which results in their failing to make the connection when it finally arrives. Or, even when the consequence is prompt, they may miss the subtlety of the connection between the result and their preceding, causal action.

Though most people believe the inherent truth of the principle of Actions Have Consequences, I am also convinced that few of them give it more than passing thought as they go about their daily affairs. The question is, why would people ignore such an all-powerful, immutable principle?

A World of Delusions

To paraphrase Robert DeRopp, man inhabits a world of delusions, which obscures reality and creates dangers for himself and others.

He rarely understands what he is doing or why he is doing it. His actions and beliefs indicate that he lives in a state of waking dreams.

When it comes to one individual deluding another, the most obvious motivation is personal gain. In some cases, the delusion involves deceit (clandestine in nature); in others, honest overzealousness (innocent in nature). But regardless of the intent, the consequences are the same: The person is deluded into believing something that isn't true. Thus, he is persuaded to ignore reality and accept an untruth in its place.

In addition to being deluded by others, there also is the problem of self-delusion. The results of this destructive practice can be devastating, ranging from mental illness to financial failure to war. Therefore, anyone serious about achieving positive results must develop the habit of carefully examining his own premises and beliefs to make certain he is not feeding himself a diet sprinkled too heavily with the spice of self-delusion.

The first step toward developing the Reality Habit, then, is to transcend our world of delusions. Delusions infest every area of life; there are no exceptions. Take the advertising business, which is the ultimate world of delusions. One might justifiably conclude that the success of most advertising is directly related to the degree to which it is able to delude the viewer, listener, or reader.

Most ads today are so ridiculous that you wonder how anyone could possibly be stupid enough to take them seriously. But obviously a lot of people do take them very seriously or companies wouldn't keep running the same idiotic ads over and over again. Advertising agencies are delightfully aware that man inhabits a world of delusions, and that it's in their financial best interests to keep feeding those delusions so customers will continue buying their products.

If you want to operate a successful advertising agency, you must remember the proven, delusionary rules of the game. For example, to sell beer, show scenes of yuppies playing touch football on the beach, jocks saying and doing illiterate things, or hardhats engaging in such intellectual activities as welding, bulldozing, or tempering molten steel. To sell liquor, show sensual women and handsome men in tuxedos hanging around fireplaces. To sell hamburgers, show frolicking adults and children who, for no apparent reason, are giddy with laughter.

People want to smell better, look better, feel better, be more sensual, work less, make more, and play more. But the reality is that people don't need beer; they don't need more greasy fries and burgers; and they certainly don't need pickup trucks that can go from zero to 150 miles an hour in three seconds. So what do advertisers do about this lack of need? They cleverly sell their products under the guise of what people *want.* Try to sell people what they need, and you're liable to end up in bankruptcy court.

On the other hand, *your* success is very much dependent upon *your* commitment to develop the habit of not straying too far from reality, so *you* don't become a victim of such delusions.

Fear of Truth
Clear back in 1982, I remembering writing an article about the coming real estate collapse, which was becoming increasingly evident at the time. In the article, I said I first began to sense a collapse was on the horizon when I heard a famous real estate guru speak at a financial seminar in the summer of 1980. In response to his own rhetorical question about when the real estate bust was going to occur, he said, with a self-assured air of finality, "Ladies and gentlemen, there's no bust. There is no bust. We have a temporary lull in the market."

I didn't mention his name at the time, because I was not interested in undermining the man or debating him. I was simply astonished that a seemingly intelligent individual would make such a naïve statement, presumably knowing the facts not only about real estate bubbles, but about the history of investment bubbles in general. The harsh reality is that, sooner or later, every investment bubble bursts.

Five years later, in May 1987, the real estate wizard who made that brash statement filed for voluntary bankruptcy, listing assets of about $1 million and liabilities of nearly $3 million. I'm not one to kick a man when he's down, which is why I'm not mentioning his name. My only purpose here is to point to his unfortunate downfall as a warning to others to be ever vigilant about falling into the trap of self-delusion.

What happens to most of us at one time or another is that we become so caught up in our own hype about our projects that we simply refuse to acknowledge any facts that fly in the face of our desires. Never forget that human beings, by and large, do not want to hear truth; rather, they try to make true that which they love. Who needs truth if it's going to put you out of business? We would much rather delude ourselves by simply ignoring the facts, even if we only succeed in prolonging the inevitable. Unfortunately, by so doing, we also guarantee disastrous long-term results.

The Something-for-Nothing Urge

The something-for-nothing urge can be seen in what I like to refer to as "the turkey markets"—the Vancouver Turkey Market, the Denver Turkey Market, and the Salt Lake City Turkey Market, to name a few of the more prominent ones. The turkey markets are where "penny stocks" are traded.

I've often said that if the slickest Wall Street trader came to Salt Lake City to ply his trade, he would have to find a new line of work. Turkey market promoters have angles that wouldn't even cross the mind of the most lecherous trader on Wall Street and gall that stretches the most larcenous of imaginations. The only reason no one's ever done a movie about the turkey markets is that moviegoers would think the story was too farfetched.

The turkey markets comprise a big game of musical chairs, with the promoters of every penny stock promising to bail out their relatives and pals at a profit as soon as the next level of turkeys buy in. Of course, we all know what happens to turkeys in the end. The only question is which ones will be left holding the fowl certificates when the music stops and there are no more buyers to be found?

A couple of years ago, when I was in New Orleans on a speaking engagement, a friend invited me to dinner with a large group of people at a plush restaurant. I was seated next to a middle-aged attorney who not only loved to talk, but also was quite inebriated (the absolute worst of all possible combinations, and just one of the many reasons why I don't drink anymore).

As the evening progressed and he continued to confide in me about one sordid deal after another in which he was involved, he began talking about a penny-stock deal that he and his cronies had recently put together. As he babbled on, he kept winking and poking me with his elbow, which I misinterpreted to be uncontrollable twitches. Finally, I realized that a wink or elbow in Cajun meant, "Y'all get what ah'm sayin', ah hope."

Nervously, I began winking back and nodding my head up and down. I managed to force a smile whenever I thought my newly found confidant was expecting one, and, while focusing on his fascinating verbiage, succeeded in getting a significant portion of my meal on my suit, white shirt, and tie. Finally, the attorney simultaneously gave me a super-duper wink and elbowing, and, with a sinister chuckle, mumbled something about "and when the stock hits the right price, the lil' old ladies end up holdin' the bag."

Ignorantly, I asked, "How do you know the price will go up? What does the company do? Is it profitable?"

The attorney looked at me with a grin that suggested he thought I was jesting, and replied, "Frien', what the company does, how much it makes or loses, and what its prospects are has nuthin' whatsoever to do with the price of the stock. The price is whatever *we* say it is. All we gotta' do is open the gates when the price is right, let the lil' old ladies in, and the rest is history."

Of course, "lil' old ladies" is just a euphemism for anyone delusional enough to invest in the penny stock of a company with no track record and no perceivable future. I never cease to be amazed at the seemingly endless pool of prospective new buyers, no matter how many *60 Minutes*–type stories air on television about penny-stock scams. Only a force as mighty as self-delusion—self-delusion based on the all-powerful, something-for-nothing urge—could make it possible for such absurd scams to continue unabated.

I found out about the realities of the penny-stock game the hard way when, in my youth, I became involved in a "public shell." I naively believed I could build the company into a legitimate moneymaking enterprise, but the promoters of the stock had other ideas. Shortly after I jumped into the water, they began hounding me to "do something" (such as make a glitzy announcement to shareholders about the prospects of the company) to aid them in raising the price of the stock.

When I steadfastly refused, they became irate and threatened to let the stock freefall. After a time, they realized I was not going to budge and, sure enough, they made good on their threat. The result was a quick and merciful burial for the company and, thankfully, an equally merciful end to a most distasteful and unpleasant experience for me.

Now, you might argue that buying a penny stock isn't really the fault of the purchaser, but, rather, the people who mislead him with false hype about the stock in question. It's important to understand, however, that such promotions wouldn't be possible were it not for the fact that people's greed motivates them to want to be deluded. They practically cry out to the scammers, "Lie to me, please lie to me." And, rest assured, there's never a shortage of blue-suede shoers around to oblige them.

If you wanted to be perverse, you might even suggest that shady penny-stock promoters provide a valuable service by telling people what they want to hear and, in the process, bursting their naive, self-delusionary bubbles. (Hmm . . . that really is perverse, isn't it?)

Regardless, the desire for something for nothing, if not kept under control, can develop into a serious case of self-delusion and completely separate an otherwise rational human being from the real world. It is therefore prudent to practice the habit of double-checking your premises before entering into any financial deal, making certain that you aren't being driven into it by a deep-seated, something-for-nothing urge.

Delusions of Grandeur

A good example of the destructiveness of having delusions of grandeur in the business world is when a person deludes himself about what he brings to the table in a negotiating situation. The person who makes this kind of mistake often ends up walking away empty-handed. If you don't have a realistic grasp of what the value of your contribution to a deal is, one of the most likely consequences is that serious people may refuse to deal with you.

At worst, you can get yourself into a catch-22 situation if the person you're negotiating with thinks your proposal is absurd. That is, in order to keep him from walking away from the deal, you might have to back down substantially, in which case the other party is likely to wonder just how much farther you might be willing to back down. And when that occurs, it puts him firmly in the driver's seat, because you've lost any semblance of posture you may have had at the outset of the negotiations.

The Egohulkster

The ultimate when it comes to delusions of grandeur can be seen in the Egohulkster, the guy who spends most of his time, energy, and money trying to convince himself and others that he's the reincarnation of Andrew Carnegie. A classic tip-off that you're dealing with an Egohulkster is lavish offices with all the trappings.

Little does he know that this kind of flash serves as a red flag to experienced, savvy entrepreneurs, particularly if the growth of his business has been unusually fast.

I remember a number of years back having dinner with an Egohulkster in his early thirties, the purpose of which was to discuss a business deal we were in the process of negotiating. We never did get around to talking business because he spent so much time yapping about who he knew, how much he made, and how clever he was. At one point, apparently sensing (erroneously) that his prey's fascination had reached a fever pitch, he blurted out, "There are three things I can do around the clock—drink, gamble, and have sex." I'm telling you, I nearly yawned.

Then, with trumpets blaring inside his arthritic brain, he went on to describe his awesome dealmaking exploits, taking care to emphasize that he regularly flitted from coast to coast on his own Learjet. Though it all sounded very impressive, when I happened to talk to one of his business associates about six months later, I was not surprised to hear that he had gone belly up.

Real-World Rule No. 52: Distrust anyone under forty with a Learjet! Years ago, I remember my nephew, who at the time was a novice stock broker working for an establishment brokerage firm, saying to me, "Uncle Robert, I can't believe it. The biggest guys in the firm cheat their own clients." I smiled and assured him that he hadn't exactly discovered the Theory of Relativity. Nevertheless, self-delusion prompted by naiveté abounds among amateur stock market players. (An amateur stock market player is defined as any person who isn't involved in the stock market on a full-time basis, yet insists on "investing" in stocks.)

Let me make it clear that I'm not talking about so-called insider trading. In fact, I don't believe there is such a thing as insider trading. Insider trading is nothing more than a figment of a bunch of regulators' imaginations. In the vague sense that the term is normally used, virtually everyone who buys stocks is guilty of insider trading. That's because all buyers, including mythical little old ladies, buy stocks based on tips (stated or implied) that someone (usually a broker) gives them about those stocks.

So what are the heavyweight market players who end up in prison guilty of? The question in itself is naive. They are, of course, guilty of ferreting out better tips! Our modern world of materialism is fueled by envy, and when you dare to play the game better than others, you run the risk of going to prison. My point is that, while there's nothing wrong with dabbling in the stock market, one must be careful not to delude himself about the realities of the game—and the realities can be pretty brutal. The guys who make big money in the market are smart, quick, and ruthless, so caveat emptor.

Developing a Correct Perception of Reality

The purpose of the above examples was to reinforce the point that major success comes only to those who develop the habit of avoiding the temptation to embrace a world of delusions. Make no mistake about it, this is a difficult task. The truth can often be harsh, and, as human beings, we quite naturally gravitate toward less pain and more pleasure. We don't like our little delusionary worlds to be upset.

However, if at times it seems inordinately difficult to refrain from embracing delusions, it's useful to remember an important principle associated with the law of Actions Have Consequences: The higher the price, the greater the benefit. The cost of a sound perception of reality is high, because the better your grasp of reality, the better the quality of your results; and the better the quality of your results, the better the quality of your life. Thus, one of the most common reasons that so few people are able to consistently achieve meaningful results is that they are unwilling to experience the discomfort associated with relentlessly pursuing a correct perception of reality.

Looking Inward

To acquire a correct perception of reality, you must, above all, develop the habit of being hard on yourself. First and foremost, you should always look to yourself for the cause of your problems, which means refusing to resort to transference. In psychology, there are many definitions of transference. When I use the term, however, I'm referring to the act of looking to people other than ourselves, or circumstances perceived to be beyond our control, for the causes of our problems.

To succeed at this task requires tremendous commitment. It also requires self-discipline, intellectual honesty, and a willingness to subordinate our delicate egos to the pursuit of long-term success. It means that no matter what someone else did to you, you must ask yourself what *you* could have done to avoid the problem. If you transfer responsibility for a problem to someone or something else, you are in effect telling yourself that you cannot prevent it from happening again because the problem is beyond your control. On the other hand, you can control any problem if you are willing to analyze it from the standpoint of what *you* can do to avoid its recurrence.

A Little Fist for the Camera, Please

A prime example of what I'm referring to happened to me shortly after my first book hit the bestseller lists. When I changed the original title of my book from *A Brutal Experiment in Business Reality* to *Winning Through Intimidation*, I hadn't given the slightest thought to the long-term consequences of my actions. I changed the title for one reason and one reason only: to gain the public's attention in the hope of increasing sales. To that end, it certainly was a success, but there was one little problem I forgot about: Actions have consequences.

The title *Winning Through Intimidation* is a book about how to *defend* yourself against intimidating people, but the editorial morticians who write for mass-circulation publications have neither the time nor the desire to read the books they write about (or, for that matter, responsibly investigate most of the things they write about). So once I had made my bed, they obligingly put me to sleep in it. Viewing the matter in this light, and considering all the juicy material I furnished them, you'd think the least the media would do is send me card on Machiavelli's birthday each year.

Early on, I had an inkling of what was to come for the remainder of at least one lifetime. *Time* magazine wanted to do a feature story about Robert Ringer and "the *Winning Through Intimidation* phenomenon," and the reporter writing the article said she needed a new photograph of me to go with the story. I agreed to allow her to send a photographer to my office, which resulted in about two hundred pictures of me in a variety of poses. With that many shots to choose from, I fully expected *Time* to select one that made me look like Paul Newman (when he was alive, that is).

No such luck. The dice had been loaded from the start. When the shooting session began, the photographer said to me, "Why don't we try to loosen you up a bit first. Just let it all hang out and make some funny faces. Here, let's see you make a fist—like this (demonstrating what he had in mind). Yeah, that's good—a fist. Great. Now, just for the fun of it, how about a few menacing facial expressions (again demonstrating what he had in mind). I've found this kind of kidding around helps reduce tension and makes for a better shooting session."

Without giving it much thought, I tried to relax and go along with the "loosening up" portion of the picture-taking session, joking with the photographer and making a fist and some contorted faces for him. Little did I know that the rest of the shooting would be purely cosmetic, because he had already gotten the pictures he was after.

Within a couple of weeks, there I was in *Time*, sporting a menacing sneer and clenching my left fist. I just happened to be looking to my left in the center of a two-page spread, and abutting my picture on the adjacent page was a photo of Michael Korda, the author of *Power!*, looking to his right. He, of course, was clenching his right fist and staring ominously "at me." I'm sure there wasn't a *Time* reader in the country who didn't assume that Korda's and my pictures had been taken together and that we willingly—even eagerly—had posed that way for the article.

The truth? Korda and I had never even met each other until we appeared together on the *Donahue* show about six months after those pictures appeared in *Time*. Nevertheless, there we were, two obvious bad guys making fists at one another and flaunting our evil ways. A nice little piece of photo editing, to say the least. Fraudulent, yes, but clever . . . very clever. The content of the story, needless to say, was even more misleading.

Now, I sometimes tend to display a soft-alloy brain—very malleable—so instead of regrouping and rationally assessing the long-term consequences of my actions, I ignorantly stumbled from one situation to another as the Ringer-the-Intimidator phenomenon caught on nationwide. *People, Us,* the *New York Times*, and local newspapers coast to coast seemed to relish every opportunity to embellish the phenomenon. Though the false hype annoyed me no end, the resulting sales of the book were gratifying, so I continued to conform to the bad-guy image the media had assigned to me.

The reason I decided to share this painful little tale with you is to make the point that it would have been easy for me to spend the rest of my life complaining that the media had treated me unfairly. But after the initial shock wore off and I was able to take the time to objectively analyze the situation, honesty compelled me to admit that the media weren't the culprits. It wasn't the media who had renamed my book *Winning Through Intimidation*, nor had they put a gun to my head and forced me to do interviews under their conditions. The power of choice had always been mine, and I had chosen not to rationally assess the long-term consequences of my actions. The resulting balloon note was a kind of permanent open season on "Ringer the Intimidator," not only by the media, but by a number of self-righteous writers and speakers who jumped at the opportunity to take potshots at me in a shameless effort to puff up their own phony images.

The most common example of transference that I see in the business world is in people who spend years believing that if only so-and-so hadn't deceived or defrauded them, they wouldn't be broke today. This kind of faulty perception of reality can spread like a cancer and result in a lifetime of failure. On the other hand, an inward-looking response can pave the way for a lifetime of success. A healthy, nondelusive reaction to someone's cheating you would be to immediately ask yourself what *you* could do to avoid dealing with such an individual in the future. The solution to a great many of your problems may be to simply improve your reading of people. And, guess what? That's something *you* can control. Such a solution isn't dependent upon others changing, which is no small point, because they almost never will.

You might say that the little picture is that someone cheated you, while the big picture is the importance of learning how to spot and avoid such a person in the future. To the extent an individual becomes adept at the latter, he begins to escape his waking-dream state and starts making strides toward entering the real world. As he forces himself to study the big picture, he becomes ever more adept at being able to observe trends in human behavior, trends that will tell him what he needs to know to avoid or successfully resolve myriad problems that stalk every person throughout life.

The Search for Truth

It can't be repeated too often: Reality and truth are synonymous. Therefore, the search for an accurate perception of reality is nothing less than a search for truth. One reason that people have differing perceptions of truth is that we all start from our own set of assumptions. Thus, the serious seeker of truth must learn to question everything and be willing to give up cherished notions, even if it means suffering discomfort.

Where does the search for truth begin? Truth is to be found in knowledge and wisdom, which are the keys to understanding how the world works. Knowledge and wisdom are the building blocks of an accurate perception of reality, and the nice thing about them is that they can never be taken from you.

Knowledge can be gained through reading, the verbal teachings of others, and even educational television programs. The more facts you know about the world, the better your chances of understanding how it works. Unfortunately, very few people are willing to commit the necessary time and effort to acquire any significant amount of knowledge.

When it comes to understanding how the world works, wisdom is even more important than knowledge. Wisdom might properly be defined as common sense or good judgment. It's easy to observe the truth in the maxim that "knowledge without wisdom is useless," because, as alluded to in the Introduction, the world is saturated with highly educated derelicts who are neither happy nor financially successful.

Learning Through the Experience of Others

Another maxim with which you are undoubtedly familiar is: Only a fool learns through his own experience, but the wise person learns through the experience of others. Obviously, learning through the experience of others is a far more efficient way of gaining wisdom, because you avoid wasting all the time, energy, and expense normally associated with learning from your own experience.

The shortest route to success in any field of endeavor, and life in general, is to seek the company of those who have more wisdom than you. It simply makes good sense to get in the habit of surrounding yourself with wise people. One very effective way to do this is to read the works of the great philosophers. This allows you to tap into a huge reservoir of wisdom that no single individual can offer. Alfred Korzybski, the renowned semanticist, described this phenomenon as "time binding," the recording of an experience and passing it on to others.

Unfortunately, no person on earth takes full advantage of the opportunity to learn through the experience of others. In fact, the actions of some people have prompted me to pen the **Contrarian Common-Sense Syndrome, which states:** *Some people consistently do the exact opposite of whatever the empirical evidence suggests would be the wisest course of action.* Perhaps you're acquainted with someone who's a victim of the Contrarian Common-Sense Syndrome and have wondered why anyone would take such a self-destructive approach to life. It's an interesting question to ponder. It could be that the person wants to prove he's smarter than those who have already experienced a similar situation; or that he doesn't really believe he deserves success; or it may just be a case of his being belligerent. It's one of those great mysteries of life that defies explanation.

Children have an especially acute problem when it comes to refusing to learn through the experience of others. It's a catch-22: Because of their inexperience, children don't have enough wisdom in the first place to understand that the easiest way to obtain wisdom is to learn through the experience of others. As a result, the Contrarian Common-Sense Syndrome can be seen in a disproportionate percentage of those passing through the Age of Infinite Wisdom, which is that blissful period of life during which a person knows everything, the unfortunate result being that his mind is pretty much closed to advice. After all, since he already possesses infinite wisdom, no one—whether he be Socrates or your average parent—can contribute much to his seemingly saturated mental bank.

Passing through the Age of Infinite Wisdom is a perfectly normal part of the maturation process, so long as it doesn't drag on for an inordinate number of years. In many cases, however, a person may remain stuck in the Age of Infinite Wisdom well into his thirties, forties, or beyond, which usually results in his continuing to act like a child long after he has become a chronological adult. Such an adult refuses to take advice from people wiser than him and can never seem to figure out why he continually self-destructs. Thus, the wise person works hard at learning through the experience of others, because he has a sincere appreciation for the efficiency of such a sound habit.

Learning Through Your Own Experience
Even if an individual wanted to, it's impossible to learn all he needs to know through the experience of others. Like it or not, each of us must gain much of our wisdom through our own experience. Which is fine, provided a person doesn't get into the habit of making the same mistakes over and over again. The longer it takes someone to learn through his mistakes, the more he runs the risk of making the Big Mistake—the mistake that can cause irreversible damage or damage serious enough to have a major, negative impact on his life.

It's imperative that you acquire the habit of extracting the lesson learned from each negative experience, then apply your newfound wisdom to future experiences. Ideally, this should become such a strong habit that when you make a mistake, you instinctively and immediately think of totally unrelated situations where correcting the underlying cause of the mistake you've just made could be applied to your benefit.

Dreams Versus Reality

While the development of a correct perception of reality is not an easy task, due in no small part to our being surrounded by a world of delusions, the nice thing about it is that you do get better with practice, provided you are committed to truth. This means being willing to subordinate your desires and wishes—your dreams, as it were—to reality.

That is not to say you should not have dreams. On the contrary, dreams are important. What it does mean, however, is that you should not allow your dreams and desires to override reality. In other words, your love of truth must be greater than your desire to make your dreams come true.

The more often, and more quickly, you are able to recognize truth in your daily life, the more likely it is that you will be in the minority of the human race that does not live in a state of waking dreams. When you correctly perceive reality, delusions begin to disappear. And as delusions vanish from your life, you are able to deal effectively with problems on a more rational basis, which in turn leads to high-level success.

As you continue to read, keep in mind that the Reality Habit is the foundation for every other million dollar habit discussed in this book. Therefore, in order for the ideas, strategies, and information I present to be of maximum benefit to you, it's vitally important that you master this foundational habit.

CHAPTER 2
THE ATTITUDE HABIT

SALT LAKE CITY, DECEMBER 3, 1969 . . .

As we began our final descent, the control tower operator—who later testified he had been on duty for sixteen hours without a break and, in addition, was nursing a bad case of the flu—told us we were two miles behind a Frontier Airlines 737 jet. Unfortunately, the truth was closer to two thousand feet. We were practically on top of it! Suddenly, our Learjet was caught in the backwash of the Frontier jetliner in front of us. It was like being hit by a tornado, and it nearly turned our small aircraft upside down.

Frantically, my pilot, Walt, shouted to the control tower, "Negative on the go-around," in response to instructions for Learjet 714-XJ to lift its nose and circle again before attempting to land. I looked up and saw the earth rushing toward us through the cockpit window. Too late to pull the nose up. The plane was almost upside down, and my five companions and I were about to crash!

The thought flashed through my mind how I had always wondered what it would feel like just before the final moment arrived. "Would I be conscious of suffering, or would it be so quick that I wouldn't even know what had happened?" I wondered. In an instant, I was about to find out.

Miraculously, Walt managed to keep the aircraft from landing upside down, but we hit at a right angle to the ground. It seemed as though we remained balanced on the tip tank of our right wing for an eternity, screeching along at 100-plus miles an hour with Walt struggling to keep the plane from flipping over on its back. Finally, the plane fell toward its underbelly and began wildly spinning in circles off to the side of the runway.

I looked down and saw gravel and dirt through gaping holes in the floor of the aircraft. Flames were shooting into the cabin as we continued to rotate like a runaway top. It's amazing how many clear thoughts can be crammed into a thimble of time when you're in a life-or-death situation. Only someone who has experienced a similar kind of disaster can fully appreciate what I mean. It's as if you instantly shift into a superconsciousness that many have described as seeing their whole life flash in front them.

I'll never know for sure how many times the Learjet spun around before coming to a halt in the muck adjacent to the runway, but it seemed like at least ten or fifteen. What I do remember is that the wheels had been torn off and the floor was almost completely gone. A single thought dominated my mind as the cabin quickly filled with fire and smoke: explosion! And instant extinction for me and the others trapped inside.

Then came those exhilarating, life-saving words from the copilot, Ron: "Emergency door!" Richard, one of my assistants who happened to be sitting in the rear seat adjacent to the emergency exit on the right side of the plane, grabbed the emergency handle and ripped the door out. All I remember thinking was that if I hurled my body through the opening quickly enough, I might have a chance to live, while a slower exit might mean death.

Without giving it a second thought, I dove out of the plane headfirst, landing like a sack of potatoes on the mixture of gravel, dirt, snow, and sleet outside. I was in my stocking feet, but who cared? Instinctively, I jumped up and began mimicking a world-class sprinter. "Got to get as far away from the explosion as possible" was my only thought as I huffed and puffed like the out-of-shape porker I was.

After about seventy-five yards, I dropped to the ground in exhaustion. I was cold and wet, but never mind that. I was alive and breathing, torn clothes and all, sitting on the frozen ground and witnessing my toy turn into an $800,000 bonfire. I watched the copilot crawl through the emergency exit, then held my breath waiting for my pilot, Walt, to follow. Two seconds, five, ten . . .

Again, an eternity, but no Walt. My gosh, Walt was going to get blown to pieces in front of my eyes! There's no way I can describe the feeling of helplessness I experienced during those tense moments. Should I run back and try to save him, John Wayne style? I pictured the next day's headlines blaring: **Jerk Entrepreneur Blown to Bits In Clumsy Effort to Save Pilot**.

Fortunately, before having to make such a life-or-death decision, Walt appeared in the emergency exit, climbed out, and ran over to me. I was still sitting on the ground, arms on knees, when he stopped in front of me. The first words out of his mouth were, "You probably don't realize it, but I just saved your life." (Ron later told me how the plane had come within a hair of flipping on its back when we were skidding along on our right wing tip, how Walt had had the presence of mind to fight the steering wheel like a rodeo cowboy atop a bull, refusing to let up until he had persuaded the out-of-control plane to come to a halt right-side up. Ron told me that if we had flipped over, it would have meant certain doom for all of us.)

It was nothing short of miraculous. The plane had been totaled, but, save for a few scratched knees, all six people aboard were uninjured. It seems strange now, but, as I sat and watched the emergency fire crews battling the blaze, I didn't give much conscious thought to the fact that I had just survived a plane crash. It's wonderful being young and ignorant—a period of your life when immortality seems certain. Why *shouldn't* I survive a plane crash?

LOS ANGELES, DECEMBER 1, 1982 . . .

A twenty-nine-year-old entrepreneur awakens before dawn to meet the challenge of a new day. Across town, a house painter goes through much the same ritual. The two men do not know each other, but, without realizing it, they will soon meet.

The young man heading east in a late-model Datsun and the painter traveling south in a Toyota pickup truck are destined to become participants in a one-in-a-million event. At approximately 6:30 a.m., just as the early morning sky is beginning to reveal a hint of color on the horizon, they arrive at a major Los Angeles intersection at precisely the same moment. Had either of them taken just one second longer to brush his teeth, put on his shoes, or start his car, he would have missed his catastrophic appointment with destiny. Unfortunately, the timing is perfect and the two men end up on the wrong side of the law of averages.

According to later accounts, both parties were traveling at speeds of at least thirty-five miles an hour, and because it was so early in the morning, there were no other cars to impede their progress. Also, the traffic light at the intersection was inoperative as a result of a severe windstorm the previous night.

One of the paramedics who arrived shortly after the accident told me he was certain the young man never knew what happened, because the Datsun left no skid marks. The pickup truck had slammed into him broadside without braking. The investigating officer told me it was one of the worst street collisions he had ever investigated.

The young man whose life had ended so abruptly had been intelligent, hard-working, and ambitious, with a great future ahead of him. Then, without warning, it was over. On December 3, 1982, thirteen years to the day after I had survived a Learjet crash, we buried my nephew.

Randomness?

The question is, why do some people, against seemingly impossible odds, escape death, while others, with the odds heavily weighted in their favor, become victims? It's a difficult puzzle for mere mortals to understand. Are cynics right in their contention that life is random? The question of whether or not man possesses the power to control his destiny—and, if so, to what extent?—has been debated throughout history.

Many people are absolutely convinced that life is random. One of their most common "proofs" is to point to the fact that so many seemingly undeserving and/or incompetent people stumble into positions of great wealth and power. Why is one man born Prince William and another an Ethiopian peasant?

Consciously or unconsciously, people who see life as completely random believe in one of two theories. The first is "quietism," which is the belief that the past, present, and future are illusions of our consciousness, but that in reality they are one and the same. In this view of the universe, nothing can be changed; everything is permanent. In other words, there's no sense trying to better one's existence, because our future existence is already history.

I've tagged the second theory the Big Bang Predestination Theory. This view of the universe holds that everything that has been, is, or will be said and done throughout history was precisely determined 14 billion years ago by the nature of the Big Bang, the initial explosion that scientists generally agree was the beginning of today's known universe. At the first instant of that spectacular eruption, every atom was sent flying on an eternal voyage that was predetermined by the intricacies of the explosion's impact. Again, this is a theory that reflects the belief that nothing can be changed by anybody or anything, i.e., every detail of every event has already been set on an unalterable course.

Predestination advocates believe that if you say, "But I can decide to pick up this salt shaker right now if I want to," not only is your free will to make such a decision an illusion, but so, too, is your belief that you think you are acting out of free will; i.e., even your perception that you made a decision was predetermined 14 billion years ago. In other words, they believe that the Big Bang propelled into the universe the atoms that formed your brain in such a way that it would think it was making such a decision today. Likewise, this one-time megablast spewed out the atoms that formed your vocal cords in such a way as to express those words today, and the atoms that formed your hand in such a way as to pick up the salt shaker today.

Human Intervention

Billionaire J. Paul Getty was once asked to write a magazine article on how he became so rich, to which he responded, "Some people find oil. Others don't." Talk about playing into the hands of randomness advocates. I acknowledge that there's a lot of luck involved in the way life turns out. But luck isn't the only factor in the equation of life, so it's unwise to depend on luck to guide your destiny.

The law of averages determines the long-term inevitability of things, i.e., it establishes odds. But here's a fascinating thing about odds: If you flip a coin, the odds, of course, are fifty-fifty that it will come up heads. Now, if you flip a coin twenty times and it comes up tails twenty times in a row, what do you think the odds are that it will come up heads the twenty-first time? Would you believe the odds are still only fifty-fifty? It's true. Ask any mathematical probabilities expert. The odds that heads ultimately will come up twenty more times than tails, and thus eventually catch up and come in line with the fifty-fifty ratio, are 100 percent. But the odds on any one flip of the coin are still fifty-fifty.

However, when it comes to the human experience, there's an important additional factor to consider. Human beings, unlike any other species, are much more than just conscious creatures. Human beings can plot, plan, conceptualize, and even will things to happen. Unlike the flipping of a coin, human beings have the capacity to alter events.

For example, a human being can decide not to flip the coin in question. He has the power of choice. He can decide to drive slower and lessen his chances of being on the wrong side of the law of averages. He can decide not to smoke and decrease his odds against dying of lung cancer. He can decide which business deal to work on and try to improve his odds of success. He can decide to stay single or get married or go skiing or just hide under his bed. And whatever decisions he makes—whatever his choices—they will have a great deal to do with *his* odds versus the inevitable, overall odds dictated by the law of averages.

To be sure, randomness and inevitability will always take their toll. But you have been given the power to intervene, to affect the odds in *your* specific case. William James was unequivocal on this point when he stated, "The greatest revolution of our generation is the discovery that human beings, by changing the inner attitudes of their minds, can change the outer aspects of their lives."

I thought about James's quote when I read Viktor Frankl's book *Man's Search for Meaning*. Frankl was a world-renowned Austrian psychiatrist who followed in the footsteps of fellow Austrians Sigmund Freud and Alfred Adler. All told, Frankl wrote twenty-eight books, lectured on almost every continent, was a guest faculty member at prestigious universities throughout the world, and was awarded numerous honorary degrees.

An impressive vitae, to be sure. Yet the most remarkable thing about Viktor Frankl is that the majority of his accomplishments came after he had spent three horrifying years in Nazi concentration camps, including Auschwitz and Dachau. In *Man's Search for*

Meaning, Frankl described, in vivid detail, the trauma, degradation, and suffering he endured during his incarceration by the Nazis. He described trudging through snow, ice, and mud, with no socks on his feet—frostbitten toes sticking through the holes in his shoes.

He recounted how the Nazis tormented him, beating him and hitting him on the back of the head with rifle butts, and what it was like to see friends and relatives stuffed into gas chambers or buried alive. Then, at the end of each brutal, agonizing day, sick from the pangs of starvation, he and his fellow prisoners would be given a cup of watered-down soup, with a single pea at the bottom of the cup, as their daily ration. He told of even having to sleep in his own excrement.

To be sure, this kind of suffering is beyond the comprehension of most people. So when someone who has endured such a living nightmare, particularly someone of Frankl's stature, reflects on his experiences, his words carry a great deal of weight. And perhaps the most fascinating reflection of all by this remarkable man who managed to survive three years of indescribable torture in Nazi concentration camps is when he stated, in *Man's Search for Meaning*, "Everything can be taken from a man but one thing: the last of the human freedoms—to choose one's attitude in any given set of circumstances, to choose one's own way."

Throughout *Man's Search for Meaning*, Frankl emphasized that attitude was an essential, shared element among those who survived Auschwitz and Dachau. I was so impressed with Frankl's emphasis on attitude as the key to his survival that it prompted me to take a closer look at the phenomenon commonly referred to as "positive mental attitude." (When Frankl spoke of attitude, the word *positive* obviously was implied; e.g., positive attitude, or the more commonly used phrase, positive mental attitude, also known as PMA.)

I am still of the opinion that most people who expound the virtues of maintaining a positive mental attitude do not have a good understanding of what it really means. When I was much younger, I was cynical about people who advocated PMA, because those who most vociferously promoted its powers often seemed to be advocating a superficial approach. I could never buy into the idea that a person could achieve positive results simply by grinning from ear to ear and telling himself, "I'm great! I can do it!"

Worse, I noted this approach often backfired over the long term. The problem is that if a person merely smiles and makes superficial proclamations about his attitude, or paints on a happy face and inundates everyone with whom he comes in contact with positive statements, he is likely to become disenchanted with PMA at the first sign of failure.

There are only five human wills: the will to power, the will to pleasure, the will to meaning, the will to self-transcendence, and the will to death. You cannot will such feelings as hope, love, or belief. In other words, those who advocate the use of motivational chants—"Just fake it till you make it" is a common one that comes to mind—only succeed in leading a lot of uninformed, naive people down a path to failure and frustration. To sustain a true positive mental attitude, to embrace permanently what I call the Attitude Habit, you must do more than just emotionalize things; you must intellectualize them. By *intellectualize*, I mean analyzing and understanding exactly what a positive mental attitude is, and how and why it works.

First, let's dispel the notion that there's anything magical about the term positive mental attitude. It's neither esoteric nor mystical. You could just as well call it a good attitude, a positive outlook, or a healthy view of things. But regardless of the name you ascribe to it, the foundation for achieving and maintaining a positive mental attitude is belief. When you say of someone, "Boy, does that guy ever have a positive mental attitude," you're really saying, "Boy, does that guy ever have strong belief."

Plain and simple, a positive mental attitude without belief is nothing more than playacting, and at the first sign of trouble, you can be certain it will desert the actor. No matter how much you insist you can accomplish something, it takes more than your insistence to make it happen. What counts is action, and only a person with a strong belief system is likely to take action.

An individual may claim to believe he can succeed in another field of endeavor, yet at the same time complain that he can't quit his present job because the risk is too great. The fact that he is not willing to risk the loss of current income demonstrates a lack of belief, thus his so-called PMA turns out to be nothing more than empty words. Through his inaction, what he is really saying is, "Golly, I might fail, and then what would I do?" Belief is an essential component of the Attitude Habit.

Acquiring the Real Thing

If belief cannot be willed, how does one acquire it? The same way he achieves an understanding of the way the world works: through the attainment of knowledge and wisdom. The greater your knowledge and wisdom, the more confident you are about your beliefs.

By knowledge, I am referring to the acquisition of specific information; by wisdom, I am referring to insight, or common sense. If you think in terms of a specific project or line of work, it's clear why knowledge and wisdom lead to belief. After all, the more you know about an undertaking or profession, the more confident you tend to be. But to achieve and maintain an overall positive mental attitude requires a much broader base of knowledge and wisdom. Specifically, it requires a solid understanding of the way the world works, as discussed in Chapter 1.

This is a vast subject, because there are an infinite number of basic principles and universal laws. However, I don't think it's necessary to be all-knowing in order to achieve and maintain a solid positive mental attitude. In fact, I've come to the conclusion that if you have a clear understanding of just four basic realities, you should be able to sustain the Attitude Habit throughout your life.

Reality Number One: Problems are an integral, ongoing part of the living experience. I don't like this any better than you do, but I'm convinced that a Pollyanna-like outlook on life is an invitation to disaster. If you see every obstacle as a totally unexpected occurrence, it's easy to delude yourself into believing that you're simply the victim of bad breaks. And if you're a victim, there's a temptation to focus on being bitter and complaining rather than taking positive action. Better to accept the reality that life is fraught with difficulties and use your time and energy to become adept at resolving those difficulties as quickly as possible.

In other words, when you intellectually and emotionally grasp the reality that problems are a way of life, you put yourself in the proper frame of mind to adapt to negative situations and maximize them to your benefit. To do this takes a genuine positive mental attitude, and realizing that life is fraught with problems actually strengthens, not weakens, your belief.

Reality Number Two: The Natural Law of Balance. The Natural Law of Balance is pretty much synonymous with Emerson's Law of Compensation. Simply put, the universe is in balance. We see it at work all around us: electrons and protons; night and day; male and female; hot and cold; life and death; two sides to a coin. Where this law comes into play in daily life is in our having to come to grips, sooner or later, with the reality that you can't have your cake and eat it, too. Nothing is one way: For every positive, there's an offsetting negative; for every negative, there's an offsetting positive.

You should never kid yourself about the reality that you must always give something up in order to gain something. If you can't see one or more offsets when making a decision, you'd best call time out and study the situation more carefully. It probably means you're overlooking one or more important facts. To ignore offsetting balances is to ignore reality, which always leads to bad long-term results.

Why is an understanding of the Natural Law of Balance so critical to the foundation of a strong belief? Because it gives you the mind-set needed to look quickly and automatically for the offsetting positive in every negative situation, which is what PMA is all about. You could make an excellent case for every negative occurrence being nothing more than an illusion hiding something of value to you. As Richard Bach put it in his book *Illusions*, "What the caterpillar calls the end of the world, the Master calls a butterfly."

You've heard this theme many times before in such expressions as "Every failure plants the seed of an equivalent success" and "Look at your glass as half full rather than half empty." People who think this way are not blind optimists. Rather, they simply understand that there's an equal and offsetting positive to every negative, so they immediately look for the positive as soon as something goes wrong. I like to refer to this habit as "maximizing the positives in negative situations."

One outstanding example involved a wheeler-dealer attorney friend of mine who had for years straddled the fence between practicing law and being an entrepreneur. He was forever lamenting about the degradation of having to practice law (you've got to love an attorney who's that candid) and resented his law practice bogging him down in trading hours for dollars. He was the sole proprietor of his firm, which included about thirty attorneys and staff members. It was an energy-draining, high-overhead situation that continually stifled his beloved entrepreneurial pursuits.

Suddenly, his whole life seemingly fell apart. He was indicted on a bribery charge regarding a cable television franchise he had worked on for one of his clients. Though adamantly proclaiming his innocence throughout the trial, to his disbelief he was convicted and sentenced to serve about three months in a minimum-security federal prison.

As a result, he was disbarred, lost about half his net worth fighting legal battles, and saw his previously pristine reputation and most of his friends disappear. His law firm, for all practical purposes, was forced to shut down because of the black cloud hanging over his head, and on the surface his future looked bleak. His life was in a shambles, but he fiercely believed in his innocence. Ultimately, his belief paid off, and his conviction was overturned on appeal.

The offsetting positive? Ironically, the result of all this devastation was that he was finally able to devote full time to entrepreneurial activities, something he had wanted to do for years. The cataclysm that had befallen him quickly accomplished what he himself had not been able to do: close down his law practice and escape the high-overhead, high-energy drain that went along with it.

By being relieved of his law-office millstone, he was able to double his already substantial net worth within a relatively short period of time. Remarkable, isn't it? What could be worse than having twenty-five years of hard work, of building an impeccable civic reputation, go down the drain because of an accusation that the courts ultimately ruled to be untrue? Yet, by ferreting out the seed of an equivalent success in the misfortune that had befallen him, he succeeded in dramatically improving all aspects of his life. It was a classic example of practicing the habit of maximizing the positives in every negative situation.

Reality Number Three: The Law of Averages. The law of averages, which I briefly touched on earlier in this chapter, can be applied to just about every facet of life.

An understanding of the law of averages is essential to the maintenance of the Attitude Habit—and certainly to financial success. If you try to put a deal together twenty times, your chances of succeeding, all other things being equal, are twice as good as they would be if you tried only ten times. And if you try forty times, your chances of succeeding are four times greater than if you tried only ten times. Now if that sounds simplistic, the question is, why doesn't everybody apply this universal law by making it a regular practice to keep on trying until they succeed? Answer: Because most people don't really understand—or don't believe—that the law of averages will work for them over the long term.

That's pretty amazing when you consider that just about everybody has read or heard about numerous success stories in which it's clear that the law of averages played an integral part in the individuals' ultimate triumphs. It's been said that Colonel Sanders approached more than one thousand restaurants before finally succeeding in getting one to carry his chicken recipe on its menu. Thomas Edison failed at inventing the light bulb more than ten thousand times. And Abraham Lincoln's story has become legend: Over a period of twenty-eight years, Lincoln lost his job, failed in business, suffered a nervous breakdown, and was defeated numerous times for public office, until he finally won the election that made him president of the United States.

The law of averages works in conjunction with the Natural Law of Balance, assuring that it's just a matter of time until the offsetting positive to any negative occurrence makes its appearance.

Reality Number Four: Through the power of the mind, it's possible to exert a great deal of control over your destiny. Interesting, isn't it? Problems are inevitable, yet through the power of your mind, you have the capacity to guide your destiny.

When Napoleon Hill, in *Think and Grow Rich*, first penned such statements as "Anything the mind can conceive and believe, it can achieve" and "When you're ready for a thing, it will make its appearance," he based his beliefs on centuries of empirical evidence drawn from human experience. But as modern scientific research has rapidly accelerated its pace, creditable cases—such as Norman Cousins' well-publicized recovery from a diagnosed terminal illness—gained more and more attention. Cousins, who ultimately passed away in 1990, was famous for his amazing mind-power cure that he described in his bestselling book, *Anatomy of An Illness.*

Cousins had a friend bring a movie projector to his hospital room and spent months watching hilarious movies like those of the Marx Brothers. As a result, he believed that he literally laughed himself out of his disease. What is particularly impressive about Cousins' case is that even his doctors agreed that his mental state was the crucial determinate in his overcoming his "incurable" illness for so many years.

Since then, scientific researchers have made dramatic strides in discovering the major role that the mind plays in producing results. Of particular interest is the research done by Dr. Karl Pribram, a neurosurgeon who has convincingly demonstrated that there is a direct correlation between what the mind visualizes and the results a person achieves. Dr. Pribram's Theory of Holographic Memory contends that the mind houses three-dimensional holographic images of what it envisions, which in turn stimulates the senses to translate those images into their physical, real-life equivalents. More precisely, when your mind believes something to be true, it stimulates your senses to draw to you the things, people, and circumstances necessary to convert the mental image it houses into a physical reality.

Thus, there is nothing at all mystical about the power of the mind to control a person's destiny. On the contrary, it's a phenomenon that is scientific in nature. Therefore, the individual who desires to achieve a *genuine* positive mental attitude (as opposed to the superficial rah-rah stuff) would be wise to study and learn how the powers of the mind can, indeed, draw to him the things, people, and circumstances necessary to convert his desires into results.

Based on the evidence, you might say that a good way to start getting what you want in life is to develop the habit of imagining that you already have it. For example, let's go back to Napoleon

Hill's statement, "When you're ready for a thing, it will make its appearance." Have you ever heard something for years, then suddenly the right person, in the right place, at the right time says it in just the right way, and you say something like, "Wow, what a great thought!" Then a friend or spouse says, "But I've been telling you that for years, and you've never gotten excited about it before. What's the big deal?"

The big deal was that prior to that time your mind was not ready to receive the information, so you didn't really believe it. Then, when it finally hit you like a sledgehammer, it was because you were at a point in your life when you were ready to hear it, ready to absorb it, ready to act on it. Thus, it created the illusion that it magically made its appearance at that particular moment.

Expansive Mental Paradigm

I use the term *mental paradigm* to describe an imaginary box within your mind, a box that houses what you believe to be the world of the possible. Conversely, everything that lies outside the perimeter of this box represents the world of the impossible to you. It's the combination of what lies both inside and outside of this imaginary box that forms what is commonly known as your "system of beliefs."

What determines on which side of the box's boundaries something lies are your experiences, your environment, your knowledge and wisdom—everything you've been exposed to throughout your life. To the extent your experiences have been positive and you possess a sufficient amount of knowledge and wisdom, not only will more possibilities lie inside the boundaries of your mental paradigm, but the paradigm itself will be expansive; i.e., your mind will be more open to new ideas, concepts, and possibilities. To the extent the opposite is true, you will tend to have a closed mind.

The more positive your system of beliefs, the more overall belief you will have in your ability to control your destiny. Likewise, the more you believe you have the power to control your destiny, the more expansive your mental paradigm will be. And the more expansive your mental paradigm, the less you are imprisoned by preconceived notions. What all this leads to is what is known as a "resourceful mind," a mind that is willing to consider virtually all possibilities.

Alternative Thinking

Resourcefulness is nothing more than alternative thinking. By alternative thinking, I mean following the habit of looking for other alternatives when confronted with problems or obstacles rather than dwelling on the fact that something didn't work out the way you had hoped it would.

This is really what PMA is all about, and it manifests itself in the form of an expansive mental paradigm. In fact, it would be appropriate to say that PMA and an expansive mental paradigm are synonymous. When your alternative-thinking mechanism is in good working order, it means your belief is strong, because it's belief that stimulates you to look for other alternatives. Belief is in great measure a result of understanding that (1) problems are a normal, integral, ongoing part of the living experience; (2) there is an offsetting positive to every negative occurrence; (3) the Law of Averages guarantees that if you just keep trying, sooner or later things will usually work out; and (4) through the power of the mind, you possess the capacity to draw to yourself the things, people, and circumstances necessary to achieve your objectives.

Did you ever experience the thrill of doing something that everyone said couldn't be done? What happened in such an instance is that you saw possibilities that others couldn't see, because your mental paradigm was more expansive than theirs.

This made you more resourceful, more attuned to alternative ways to accomplish your objective. Rather than saying that when you were ready for it, the solution made its appearance, it might be more appropriate to explain it as breaking through the existing boundaries of your mental paradigm and discovering what was outside. In other words, you discovered possibilities that originated beyond the existing perimeter of your mental paradigm.

Further, since it's impossible to know all the possibilities that exist outside of our mental paradigms, our limitations, theoretically speaking, are pretty much where we choose to place them. What an exciting thought. Talk about being able to write your own lifeticket . . . this is it.

Anything but my Mercedes!
I remember a Beverly Hills acquaintance of mine once lamenting about his financial problems, and my asking him why he didn't sell either his wife's or his Mercedes to ease his burden. Ouch! You would have thought I shot him through the heart: "Sell my Mercedes! Are you kidding? I couldn't do that."

"Why not?" I asked.

"I couldn't sell my Mercedes. What would people in Beverly Hills think? I'd be ruined."

At that particular time, selling one of his Mercedes was not part of this individual's world of the possible. It was a thought that lay outside the perimeter of his mental paradigm, and thus was not an alternative that his unresourceful state of mind would consider. Note that I said "at that particular time." The resourcefulness of most people tends to change with changing circumstances. For example, what if this same individual had suddenly found himself in a jail cell in Mexico, and a guard said to him, "I'll tell you what. If you sell your two Mercedes, I'll get you out of here." Under those circumstances, his response might very well have been, "Sell them? Are you kidding? You can have them for free!"

The moral is that to achieve consistently positive results, it's important to consistently practice the habit of maintaining an expansive mental paradigm. If you wait until you're desperate before considering unconventional or extreme alternatives, that's probably how you'll live the remainder of your life—desperate.

Unlimited Control?

As I said, our limitations, theoretically speaking, are pretty much where we choose to place them. I use the term *theoretically*, because a positive mental attitude doesn't give you omnipotence. But to the extent the Attitude Habit becomes a way of life for you, one thing is certain: You can do everything *better*. Viktor Frankl's positive attitude didn't guarantee his survival in Auschwitz and Dachau, but it did guarantee that his odds would be much better than if his mind had been negative regarding the possibility of survival.

Put another way, while we are never free from the inevitabilities of life—illness, accidents, natural disasters, and the like—we *are* free to choose our attitude toward them. And in so doing, we can at a minimum swing the odds in our favor and dramatically increase our chances of success—which, of and by itself, is sufficient reason to work hard at nurturing the Attitude Habit every day of your life.

CHAPTER 3

THE PERSPECTIVE HABIT

It was exactly 8:10 p.m. on March 18, 1988, as Mexicana flight #913 touched down on the runway at the Manzanillo airport. I stared out the window into the darkness, wondering whether my decision to make Mexico my home for the next year had been an impulsive one. I had felt like this was the ideal time to get away, erase from memory the peoplewebs that clouded my once-clear mind, do some writing in peace and quiet, and reevaluate that unpredictable and mysterious experience called life.

My wife was almost six months pregnant, but I had rationalized that if there were any problems, we could always get to Guadalajara by air in less than a half hour. And, who knows, maybe the medical facilities in the Manzanillo area weren't quite as bad as people had led me to believe. The tentative plan was to come back to the United States after my wife reached her eighth month, have the baby, then return to Manzanillo to finish out the year.

Besides, for once in my life, the timing was perfect. The right situation had presented itself at exactly the right time. About eight years earlier, a friend of mine had built a palatial, 25,000-square-foot villa on a mountaintop just above the Las Hadas Hotel (where the movie *10* was filmed), but his business activities had kept him from spending much time there in recent years.

Anyone who has been an absentee homeowner in Mexico knows what that means—problems. So it was a genuine value-for-value situation: We struck a bargain whereby my wife and I agreed to live in the villa for about a year and watch over things, try to instill some esprit de corps in the villa's staff, and get the administration of the place under control. Seemed like a simple enough task. (If you've ever lived in Mexico, that last statement undoubtedly has you smiling and gently shaking your head from side to side.)

To live in Mexico is like enrolling in Problem Solving 401. It's the ultimate test of one's resourcefulness. During our first week at the villa, we experienced a few "minor inconveniences": The water throughout the villa turned dark brown; then, it went off completely for two days, which meant none of the toilets could be flushed; we found supersized rats in our kitchen, along with the expected cockroaches, lizards, and assorted dinosaur bugs; the air-conditioning went off for several days, which made the solid concrete rooms feel like hermetically sealed tombs; and the telephones dropped dead two or three times. Of course, none of this could mean much to you if you've never lived in Mexico and tried to get a repairman to come and fix something.

Our villa was on Manzanillo Bay, about fifteen miles from the city of Manzanillo. We were actually closer to a couple of small pueblos, Santiago and Salahua, than Manzanillo. On our second day at the villa, we felt mentally prepared to take on Santiago and shop for groceries. Had someone told us in advance that Camacho's was the absolute worst grocery store in Mexico, it still would have been a shock. That, however, was not what we had been told. We had been assured that Camacho's was by far the *best* market in the area. As I casually strolled into the store, I took one look and immediately began scouring my mind for an appropriate one-liner. It was no use; my mind went blank.

The worst-stocked, shabbiest corner grocery store in any ghetto in the United States would be a gourmet market in Santiago.

The only place where I had seen less food on store shelves was in Leningrad, and the customers in Leningrad were somber. But in Camacho's, people were actually smiling. I figured there must be something I didn't understand, so I started smiling, too. I made up my mind, then and there, that it was going to be a long year and that I had two choices: I could complain and suffer like a normal American, or I could adapt to the locals' way of life.

It wasn't long before I actually began to look forward to going to Camacho's a couple of times a week to shop and exchange "Spanglish" quips with Mr. Camacho and his employees. What a great occasion when the weekly issue of *USA Today* arrived or the store's refrigerator was fully loaded with a new shipment of Pepsi. It's all a matter of how one framed the situation in his mind.

After a couple weeks of working hard to adapt to a radically new lifestyle, my wife and I settled down to a relaxed pace the likes of which I had never before experienced. We walked on the beach, read a lot, went to the Saturday open-air market in Santiago, fixed up the villa, and even ventured into the city of Manzanillo to shop. On balance, it was delightful, notwithstanding our paranoid concerns about irritable scorpions hiding under the bedcovers, anxiously awaiting the arrival of our toes.

However, our new way of life was also taking a toll on my wife. For one thing, the villa was so big and had so many stairs that it was the equivalent of a hard workout just to get through a normal day. Also, the streets and roads in much of rural Mexico were not built with pregnant women in mind. The road up the mountain to our villa consisted primarily of jagged rock, and most of the several miles up and down the mountain had to be covered at speeds of no more than ten miles an hour. And even at that pace, you felt as though you were riding atop a wild bronco—in slow motion. The streets of Santiago were a mixture of large stones and dirt and were even bumpier than our mountain road.

It was mid-April. The baby was not due until early July, but, to be on the safe side, I thought it would be a good idea to see what medical facilities existed in the area in the unlikely event an emergency should arise. We asked several people, both Americans and locals, about the childbirth facilities and medical treatment available in the area, and the consensus seemed to be that "no one has their babies in Manzanillo." There simply were no available medical facilities as we know them in the United States. In a true emergency, a last-ditch hope, we were told, was the Naval Hospital in the small town of Las Brisas, about ten miles away.

The next Sunday we took a drive to check out the Naval Base facility in person. Again, culture shock. We didn't need to go inside. One look at the outside and you knew that no one with any serious medical problem gets out alive. My first words were, "Well, so much for emergencies in Manzanillo. No one has a baby here and lives to tell about it. At least we can totally eliminate this as an alternative, emergency or not." We laughed and joked about it as we pulled away in our car, wondering how people survive in makeshift hospitals like this all over the world. Scary. Being an American has got to be the most sheltered, secure life on the planet.

As I lie in bed that night, staring at the ceiling, my thoughts kept coming back to what we had seen at the Naval Base. "Suppose . . . what if . . . no, unthinkable." I wouldn't even allow myself to consider the possibility. I simply couldn't let it happen, no matter what. I made up my mind that we had better plan to head for the United States around the end of May, just to be on the safe side. Then, after all was well with the baby, we could return to Manzanillo around the third week of July.

I felt relieved at my decision, though my wife kept insisting that it really wasn't necessary to leave for the States so early. Unfortunately, her condition didn't give credence to her protests, because she gradually was experiencing more and more discomfort. Each trip up and down the bumpy mountain road seemed to be tempting the fates, until finally I made most of the treks into town alone in order to spare her the wear and tear. This created somewhat of a problem, because my wife spoke fluent

Spanish, while I spoke practically none. Try that in the middle of Mexico if you want to find out what real insecurity is.

By the end of the first week in May, my wife's condition was deteriorating at an accelerating pace, and I seriously began to think in terms of emergencies. I decided we had better get to Guadalajara within the next week in order to have her checked out at a good medical facility, then decide whether to come back to Manzanillo, stay in Guadalajara until the baby was born, or try to make it back to the United States. Unfortunately, Aeromexico had just gone broke, and that left only Mexicana Airlines' two flights a week to Guadalajara as our single source for air travel.

Worse, we were informed that international law would not permit a woman to fly if she was more than seven months pregnant. To top that off, all flights to Guadalajara were fully booked for weeks to come. It was getting to be a very unfunny situation. My anxiety heightened as I tried to assess our options rationally.

I looked into renting a van and found that it would be a six-hour drive, assuming no problems en route (always a bad assumption in Mexico), and very uncomfortable in many stretches along the way. "Would she be able to make it?" I wondered to myself. I had no choice; I'd have to try. The vision of the so-called hospital in Las Brisas kept pushing me forward, forcing me to select from among the unpleasant alternatives available to us.

I reserved a van for Saturday, May 13, and began packing our necessities. In the meantime, I had the responsibility for making sure the staff was taking care of the villa, the payroll was being met, and the whole place wouldn't come apart at the seams as soon as we left. I had come to Mexico to relax and write, but circumstances were changing rapidly. What did I know from gardeners and housekeepers who didn't speak English? Worse, the air-conditioning had now stopped functioning altogether and needed to be completely overhauled or perhaps replaced. In addition, the water was periodically shutting off, and the car was on the verge of breaking down.

My wife was in such pain by Wednesday afternoon that we decided to set up an appointment to see a doctor in Manzanillo on Thursday, just to make sure we weren't taking a life-or-death risk driving to Guadalajara on Saturday. Through a friend of ours, Captain Eugenio Gutigrez, we secured an appointment with Dr. Abrajan, who examined my wife on Thursday morning. Dr. Abrajan told us that my wife definitely would not carry the baby full term, but probably would not deliver for another month or so. He also diagnosed a huge, excruciatingly painful bulge in her upper-left abdomen as a hernia. Nevertheless, it was his opinion we should be able to make it to Guadalajara by van, assuming my wife didn't get any worse by Saturday.

That evening, however, things did take a turn for the worse— much worse. As the night progressed, my wife began writhing in pain and screaming in anguish. This was a woman who never complained and who had a very high threshold of pain. As she became more and more uncontrolled, reality began to set in. This was not a nightmare; it was not a movie; it was not something I was reading about in the newspaper. It was happening to *us*. The ultimate emergency that every civilized person has had nightmares about was here and now. Guadalajara was no longer an option. The only question was what was going to happen right here in Manzanillo!

I called Hans Rothlisberger, our best friend in Mexico, who was public relations director at the Las Hadas Hotel next door. He had been monitoring our situation closely for the past couple of weeks, so he was aware that things were not going well. When he heard my wife's screams in the background, he immediately set in motion a Mexican chain reaction by calling our mutual friend, Andy Shryer, who in turn called Captain Gutigrez, who in turn called the Red Cross and Dr. Abrajan.

Within thirty minutes, the Red Cross arrived, carried my wife out on a beat-up stretcher, and put her in an old truck-ambulance. Then we started down the mountain over the bumpy, rocky road we had come to know so well. I sat next to my wife in the ambulance and held her hand tightly. Hans followed behind in his car as we made our way—at a pace of about two miles an hour—down the long mountain road, with my wife moaning in pain.

As the old ambulance bounced up and down unmercifully, the Red Cross doctor told my wife it would be necessary to examine her on the way to the hospital. I watched his face closely as he proceeded with the examination and immediately saw that something was wrong. He spoke to my wife in Spanish, and she relayed his words to me: "You're going to have this baby *tonight*."

"Impossible," I thought. "It can't be happening. Not here . . . not in Manzanillo. Not two months premature . . . not at the Naval Hospital." It was only a few weeks ago that we were laughing about how we could never consider the Naval Hospital as a viable alternative. Now I just wanted to awaken from my nightmare. I wanted to clamp magic wings on my wife and me and zip off to Guadalajara where we would be safe from the unknown. Somehow, some way, I just couldn't allow it to happen. But the reality was that it *was* happening. One of those inevitabilities of life was upon us. We were headed toward the Naval Hospital, where the fate of my wife and unborn child would soon be decided.

As the ambulance ended its bumpy journey down the mountain road and settled onto the old highway en route to Las Brisas, all I could see through the dirty windshield was a kaleidoscope of darkness, beat-up cars, people occasionally darting across the road, and smoke from the day's burning of fields that had settled over the highway. The siren on our vehicle droned in my ears as I tried to picture the events that lay ahead.

When we finally arrived at the Naval Hospital, the staff immediately prepared my wife for delivery, then wheeled her into the labor room. I was told to stay behind a three-foot-high wall about a dozen steps from the room. In the sweltering humidity, I paced the floor for hours, grimacing at my wife's every moan and scream. Throughout the night, my mind gyrated wildly in an attempt to project all possible scenarios. As I continued my automaton-like pacing, I reflexively swatted mosquitos and watched cockroaches scoot in front of me on the floor without so much as a pause.

No one, I thought to myself, knew so little about childbirth as I did. I wondered what the odds were of a two-months-premature baby surviving under the *best* of circumstances. I had no idea. Even more important, what were a premature baby's chances under the *worst* of circumstances? Horrible thoughts bombarded my mind nonstop, and my head pounded as my wife's screams became louder and more desperate.

Finally, at about 2 a.m., Dr. Abrajan came out of the labor room and approached me with a somber expression on his face. He said something in Spanish that I didn't understand, then motioned for me to get Hans, who had been sleeping in his car outside. As I rushed out to the car, I thought to myself, "The baby is dead. The baby died." I could only hope that my wife was all right. After waking Hans, he and I hurried back inside where Dr. Abrajan began talking to him. About a minute elapsed before Hans turned to me and explained, in a grim and sympathetic tone, that they had tried several times to get the baby out, but each time they had started to lose his heart beat. The umbilical cord was apparently wrapped around his legs. There was only one hope: a caesarian operation.

I grimaced and bit down hard on my lower lip. This was no nightmare, and there were no fairytale wings with which to make a movie-ending escape to Guadalajara. Zero hour had arrived; the cataclysm was upon us. There would be no reprieve. I was handed a document to sign—written in Spanish, of course—and a pen. It's the moment every human being fears will arrive one day, a matter of life or death over which he has absolutely no control. The heat . . . the humidity . . . the mosquitos . . . the cockroaches . . . a dying baby who's never seen the world . . . a beloved wife screaming just a few feet away . . . a foreign-language document to be signed. There are situations in life where the choices ultimately come down to terrible or worse. In this case, the terrible choice was to sign the document. The worse choice was certain death—perhaps two deaths.

As they wheeled my wife into the hall toward the operating room, she called to me in a barely audible tone, "I love you, Robert." Tears streamed down my face as I responded, in a badly cracked voice, "I love you, too, Ester." I watched as they rolled her down the hallway, thinking to myself that I may never again see alive the kindest, most sensitive, loving, compassionate human being I had ever known. The fate of the most important person in my life was now completely out of my hands, controlled by strangers in a Third World country. "How could I possibly have allowed us to get into this kind of situation?" I asked myself.

Two nurses who had been sleeping on cots jumped up and rushed into the operating room after my wife, and the doors shut behind them. The wait was on. I had almost two hours to replay three possible scenarios in my mind, all of them horrifying: My wife might live, and the baby die; my wife might die, and the baby live; or both my wife *and* the baby might die. I was reeling emotionally, still clinging to the hope that I would wake up and find that none of this was really happening. One moment I would find myself trying to comprehend how I could possibly cope with the third and worst of all possible scenarios; the next moment my mind would completely quit on me, incapable of thinking the unthinkable.

The apocalypse continued: There was no general anesthetic available, and it took forty-five minutes of prying and sticking for the anesthesiologist to get the local anesthetic into my wife's spine. At one point, she stopped breathing, but they were able to bring her back just in time. As she laid on the operating table, her insides exposed, she was able to witness the entire operation in the mirror above her. It was a tense, monumental struggle, but the doctor finally succeeded in pulling the baby from her with a force so great that it lifted her entire body off the table.

Finally, at 4:12 a.m., the doors to the operating room flung open and out charged a young doctor, surgical mask covering his face, carrying the baby in a frayed towel-like cloth. He was moving fast, and went right by me on the way to an antiquated incubator behind a glass divider wall. The baby wasn't crying, but he was breathing—barely. As the doctor tried to get the baby into the incubator, he accidentally knocked the lid off, and it fell directly onto the baby's face. Again, I bit hard on my lower lip as I watched the scenario unfolding just a few feet away from me.

Unable to properly adjust the top of the incubator, the young doctor picked up the baby, carried him down a hallway, and took him into another room that housed several more empty incubators. In the meantime, a nurse came out of the operating room and assured me that my wife was going to be all right, so I hurriedly followed the young doctor. In the intensive care room, he began frantically working on the infant in an effort to keep him alive. It occurred to me that if the baby didn't make it, I might never know what he looked like, so when the doctor seemed to have things somewhat under control, I hesitatingly asked if it would be possible for me to see my infant son up close. Reluctantly, the doctor allowed me to take a quick look.

That moment will forever live in my memory. The poor little guy was struggling for every breath he could snatch and barely had enough strength to eke out an occasional, almost inaudible cry. Nevertheless, premature and all, he was absolutely beautiful. Dr. Chagoya, the doctor who had rushed him out of the operating room, explained that the baby's respiratory system was poorly developed, and that it would be a touch-and-go situation, particularly during the first twenty-four hours. Infection, pneumonia, heart failure—everything was a danger at this point. Crude as their equipment was, the medical staff got the baby hooked up to a respirator, inserted breathing tubes into his trachea, planted an intravenous feeding tube in his left arm, and began working on him methodically.

After Hans finally departed for the hotel, I continued to pace the sweltering, quiet corridors of the hospital—thinking . . . thinking . . . thinking. Hour after hour I paced, swatting the mosquitos that relentlessly stalked me. As my mind floated aimlessly, it kept coming back to two words, *perspective* and *relativity*. At a time like this, I thought to myself, how petty and inconsequential most of the day-to-day problems of life seem. All the little slights, the hurts, the injustices, the bad breaks, the financial losses we experience as we stumble through life in our waking state of dreams seem so unimportant when viewed in a relative light. When juxtaposed against the life or death of someone whom we dearly love, how absurd they seem.

Each time I passed the intensive care room, Dr. Chagoya was standing over my son, watching his every movement, adjusting the maze of tubes sticking out of him, massaging his hands and feet, administering oxygen to him intermittently, checking his heart rate and pulse, and, above all, never taking his eyes off him. Whenever Dr. Chagoya looked up and saw me, he spoke with his eyes. He is one of the most compassionate young men I've ever known, someone who really cares.

At about 8 a.m., another young doctor, Dr. Hector Americo Bautista, relieved Dr. Chagoya. I was concerned, but not for long. Again, seemingly infinite compassion. Once when Andrew's heart stopped beating, Dr. Americo alertly sprang into action and quickly got it pumping again by rapidly massaging it. This remarkable young man stood by the baby's incubator for twenty-four hours without taking a single break—adjusting tubes, massaging, and always watching . . . watching . . . watching.

In the midst of a horrendously insecure situation, there was one thing about which I felt totally secure: What Mexican physicians lack in facilities, equipment, and technology, they more than make up for with compassion, care, and concern. It is impossible for me to describe the bond I felt with these men. I was truly touched by their professionalism and compassion. Many may have the intellect to practice medicine, but only a small percentage have the character to practice people-medicine. We were most fortunate to have on our side a number of these extraordinary people-medicine doctors, the finest I could ever hope to meet in my lifetime.

These compassionate, caring doctors, together with a number of equally compassionate, caring nurses, painstakingly brought my wife and son back from the brink of death. What began as an ordeal of nightmarish proportions evolved into nothing short of a miracle. In less than a week, both my wife and the baby stabilized, and we were able to return to the villa together. On that fateful night a week earlier, we had left the villa as two; we easily could have returned as one; instead, we returned as three. That which almost ended our lives made us infinitely stronger and certainly gave me a much healthier perspective of my own little world.

Problems Relative to What?

My family's brush with disaster in Mexico was the most difficult course I have yet to take at the University of Life, and undoubtedly the most important. To say the least, it dramatically changed my perspective on life. Since the Mexico experience, many things I once looked upon as serious problems have been relegated to minor status or, in many cases, I don't think of them as problem at all.

The inability to view day-to-day problems in a relative light is a widespread human defect that can be the difference between success and failure. To be sure, we all have problems, but it's important to develop a mind-set that prevents you from blowing them out of proportion. You will find routine problems in your life to be much less burdensome if you can cultivate the Perspective Habit. By *perspective*, I'm talking about the capacity to view things on their relative level of importance. When problems arise, get in the habit of asking yourself: problems relative to what?

Once we escape the Age of Infinite Wisdom, experience teaches us how quickly yesterday's garbage can become today's delicacy. Today we're passed over for a promotion and think the world is coming to an end. Tomorrow we lose our job, and a promotion is no longer important to us; we just yearn to have our job back. Then we lose our health, and suddenly we realize how good we had it when our only problem was not having a job. Truly, all problems are relative.

In this regard, financial problems are at the top of most people's lists. Most of us have difficulty grasping the reality that no matter how bad our financial problems may be, no one is going to drag us outside, put us against a wall, and execute us. Don't get me wrong. I don't mean to imply that financial problems can't be serious, and I certainly know, as evidenced by my family's saga in Mexico, that from time to time each of us does come face to face with perilous problems. But what I am suggesting is that rather than magnify daily problems, a person is much ahead of the game if he uses the relatively small number of genuinely serious problems he has to keep run-of-the-mill problems in proper perspective.

The Catastrophe Illusion

As I pointed out in the previous chapter, it's important to come to grips with the fact that problems are an integral, ongoing part of the living experience. Life is a never-ending stream of hardships, obstacles, rejection, frustration, and so-called bad luck. Life is lost jobs, loans that aren't granted, sales that don't close, people who treat you unfairly, and deals that fall through at the last minute. None of these things are fatal; they're just life.

It's absolutely essential that a person grasp this reality if he is serious about developing the Perspective Habit. Likewise, it's essential to absorb the truth contained in the Natural Law of Balance, as discussed in Chapter 2. If you believe there is an offsetting positive to every negative occurrence—which there is—you should make it a high priority to cultivate the habit of quickly and automatically maximizing the positives in every negative situation.

As a matter of fact, all four of the realities I discussed in the previous chapter as the foundation for developing and maintaining a strong positive mental attitude are equally important to maintaining a healthy perspective. (To refresh your memory, the four realities are: [1] problems are a normal, integral, ongoing part of the living experience; [2] there is an offsetting positive to every negative occurrence [the Natural Law of Balance]; [3] the Law of Averages guarantees that if you just keep trying, sooner or later things will usually work out; and [4] through the power of the mind, you possess the capacity to draw to yourself the things, people, and circumstances necessary to achieve your objectives.) Remember, understanding these four realities is what gives you the belief necessary to maintain a true positive mental attitude, and PMA is an essential catalyst for breeding and practicing the Perspective Habit.

The Great Illusion Known as Misfortune

It's also important to understand that the offsetting positives to any negative situation not only can be subtle in nature (i.e., the association to the original negative may not always be apparent), they may not appear until a much later date or may appear in small increments over a long period of time.

Put another way, misfortune and setbacks are often, if not always, nothing more than illusions, because we fail to connect the long-term benefits to the negative occurrence. To demonstrate the subtle, long-term, offsetting payoff that can be traced back to a perceived disaster, I'm reminded of a story that a now-deceased friend of mine once told me. He said that during the Great Depression, he lost his house when he couldn't keep up his mortgage payments to the bank. Because of that traumatic experience, he vowed he would never again borrow money, and he conducted both his business and personal affairs within the framework of this policy throughout the remaining fifty years of his life.

He ultimately accumulated a net worth of $500 million, and attributed much of his success to his financial staying power during bad times. With his large cash reserves, he was able to buy everything from land to precious metals at depressed prices, then hold on to them for the long-term payoff. He paid cash for everything he bought—from cars to homes, from office equipment to whole companies—never owing a penny to anyone. As a result, he was able to weather numerous recessions completely unscathed.

By contrast, think of how millions of people have reacted to foreclosures on their properties. You see them on television all the time. The major networks love to parade irate farmers in front of the cameras, who see foreclosure as the end of the world and are intent not on maximizing the positives in their negative situations, but on expending their energies on bitterness and blaming their problems on others. It's not a matter of lacking compassion for these people; it's a question of their own lack of perspective blinding them to solutions and/or offsetting benefits to their dilemmas. The difference between these people and my wealthy friend is that he used what he had learned from a seemingly catastrophic situation to lay the groundwork for a personal fortune.

Since my friend pointed out to me the subtle connection between his long-term mega-success and a painful experience in his life, I've made it a point to closely observe many other heavyweight successes to see if I could spot a trend. I have. In fact, it's much more than a trend. I am convinced that every successful person keeps his problems in proper perspective and makes it a habit to search immediately for the offsetting positives in every negative situation. The truly successful individual practices the Perspective Habit by seeing adversity as both a learning experience and a masked opportunity.

High Stakes

To come out ahead in situations where a lot is at stake and emotions are running high, the skilled negotiator, like the skilled card player, is adept at knowing when to discard. And to be good at the art of knowing when to discard, you must maintain a healthy perspective. A healthy perspective makes it possible for you to intellectually and emotionally understand that no deal is a life-or-death matter. With such a perspective as a backdrop, it's then much easier to lay down "either-or" ultimatums.

In other words, by keeping money situations in proper perspective, you're able to objectively set limits in advance, then stick by them. Your perspective should always be that the best deal in the world comes along every day. If you aren't able to cultivate such a perspective, the likely result is that you'll yield points or dollars to the other side as the negotiating heats up. This sets the stage for an atmosphere somewhat analogous to blackmail; i.e., much like the problem of overestimating what you bring to the negotiating table, the more the other guy sees you giving in, the more he assumes you will continue to give in. And once the ball starts moving in that direction, it's extremely difficult to slow its momentum.

To lessen your chances of getting caught in this trap, the first step is to keep money in proper perspective. Making money is important, and making deals is an important key to making money. It therefore logically follows that closing deals is important. Nevertheless, the importance of money is relative. To the extent you fail to see financial situations in a relative light, you're likely to press. And the more you press, the less likely you are to come out ahead. When you begin to feel as though emotion is overtaking you in a negotiating situation, get in the habit of stepping back and, first of all, reminding yourself that your life isn't literally at stake on the outcome. Second, practice the habit of reevaluating the facts, and make certain you aren't allowing a lack of perspective to take you beyond the bounds of prudent action.

How's Your Blood Pressure?

When it gets down to it, I believe one of the main reasons we have such difficulty seeing our everyday problems in a relative light is that we take ourselves too seriously. There's a fine line between pathos and humor, and one of the many advantages that a human being has over every other species is that he possesses the capacity to detach himself both from situations and from his own self. And one of the unique ways in which he is able to accomplish this is through the use of humor. Man is the only "animal" who can laugh at himself. He can choose not to see every problem, every unfair act, and every negative situation as monumental in importance.

For example, everyone knows what it feels like to be wrongly accused or slandered. Sometimes it's enough to make you want to stop people on the street and force them to listen to your tale of woe: "Justice must be done at any cost! The accusations are false, I tell you! The world is unfair!" Alas, though, no one cares. We get so caught up in our hurt, so upset over being wronged, that it can be very difficult for us to look beyond our fragile little egos and put seemingly unfair situations in proper perspective. Nonetheless, it's important to make it a habit to cut through your emotional gridlock, step back, and see the perceived wrong in relative terms. When you do so, you'll find it absolutely amazing what it can do for your results, efficiency, quality of life, self-esteem, and longevity, among other things.

It's pretty widely accepted in the medical profession that it's not stress that kills people, but how they react to it. Man has the capacity intellectually and emotionally to grasp the reality that life is imperfect. To the extent one succeeds in embracing this reality, he becomes known as an imperturbable person. Have you ever known someone who's imperturbable—blood pressure 22 over 8? It can be maddening to deal with such an individual. But the rewards to the imperturbable person can be enormous, because he holds a tremendous advantage over those who are fast on the emotional trigger. The more distraught you allow yourself to become, the more energy you waste and the less likely you are to make sound decisions that lead to positive results.

Perhaps, worst of all, the individual who doesn't develop the habit of maintaining his composure through a healthy perspective also runs the risk of losing the confidence of others. First, because it weakens his posture; second, because he makes obvious errors in judgment.

So What?

Perhaps the most important point to draw from this chapter is that life's endless problems and seeming injustices need not prevent a person from achieving his goals. Your success is very much dependent upon your ability to cope with problems—to maximize the positives in negative situations—and one of the best catalysts for accomplishing this is to learn to keep things in proper perspective.

Give this some serious thought the next time you feel as though you're the victim of some terrible injustice—like being bumped from a flight for which you've had a confirmed reservation for a month. Embrace the habit of repeatedly asking yourself the tough, rational-perspective question: *So what?*

"But there's no other flight out tonight."

"So what?"

"But I'll have to take a morning flight, and I'll be an hour late for my meeting."

"So what?"

"But it may blow the deal."

"So what?"

Save your serious concerns for genuinely serious situations, such as the Mexico experience I described at the outset of this chapter. Mastering the Perspective Habit allows you to see your day-to-day problems—especially all the petty injustices you feel have been done to you—in a more relative light. If you work hard at cultivating the Perspective Habit, it will pay enormous dividends to you throughout life.

The next time you find yourself acting as though the world is coming to an end, remember that only one time in history is such an event going to take place, and I have news for you: You won't be around to remember it happening anyway.

So get in sync with the Perspective Habit and . . . take it *eeeasy*.

CHAPTER 4

THE PRESENT LIVING HABIT

I was taking a late afternoon stroll on Ocean Avenue in Newport Beach, California, sorting my thoughts and occasionally checking the progress of the slowly setting sun. I don't recall exactly how it happened, but, through a quirk of fate, I found myself engaged in conversation with a complete stranger, which was quite out of character for me.

For whatever reason (perhaps the work of the Cosmic Catalyst?), we seemed to have a common communication channel that was instantly recognizable to both of us. I had noticed Dan pacing above the cliffs a couple of days before, obviously deep in thought, just as he was today. As the conversation unfolded, he said to me, "You know, I've been searching for a long time for a feeling I experienced many years ago. I was a whiz-kid stockbroker, on top of the world financially, until my early thirties. Then, one day, I suddenly realized that I wasn't happy, and, to the disbelief of my colleagues, I abruptly quit."

"Did you know what you wanted to do when you quit? Did you have another business in mind?" I asked.

"I really had no idea what I wanted to do. All I was sure of was that I was sick of the proverbial rat race, sick of the money worshipping, sick of the win-at-all-costs mentality of the people I worked with day in and day out—sick of the business world in general. I just wanted to get as far away from the money jungle as possible and have the opportunity to reflect on my life.

"I bought a quaint, aging little house in a modest neighborhood, packed away my suits, dress shirts, and ties, and bought several pairs of overalls. At first, I spent most of my time fixing up the house and just treating my mind to some long-overdue relaxation. Then, after a while, I started making stained-glass windows in my garage and selling them to people in the neighborhood. I couldn't recall my ever enjoying anything quite so much. I sometimes found myself chuckling about the drastic change in my lifestyle. It was hard to believe—me, the hotshot wonder boy of the brokerage business, wearing overalls, working with my hands, and making stained-glass windows."

"Is that what you miss now—making stained-glass windows?" I inquired with a growing fascination about Dan's background.

"It was much more specific than that—the point in time, that is. I remember that I had finished my work for the day, I was wearing overalls, and I was sitting on the front steps of my house. It was spring, and there was a warm breeze blowing in from the ocean. I can't adequately describe what I felt, except that my mind was completely relaxed—the only time in my life I could remember that happening to me. Then, suddenly . . . it's hard to put into words . . . I experienced this feeling of contentment taking over my entire body, a sensation of total joy. I was conscious of wanting to freeze that moment in time and live in that contented state for eternity."

The soft smile on his face slowly faded as he looked toward the ocean and continued, "For fifteen years now, I've been searching, hoping to recapture that feeling of ecstasy . . . searching for it . . . believing it's out there somewhere . . . but it always seems beyond my reach . . . beyond . . ." At that point, his voice trailed off to a barely audible whisper.

Dan had described his journey through adulthood so vividly, distilled the essence of his life in such sensory detail, that I felt as though I had experienced it firsthand with him. Somewhat hesitant to cause him any undue anguish, I quietly pressed on with my inquiry. "Why do you think you've never been able to recapture that unique feeling of contentment and joy? What do you think it was?"

"You know, it's so obvious now, but at the time I didn't see it coming. Little by little, working away by myself in my garage, the demand for my stained-glass windows increased, until finally I had to hire an assistant. Success led to more success, until I found myself with a number of employees on the payroll and had to move my business to a commercial building. I didn't realize what I had lost until it was too late. It's as though I had awakened from a dream and found myself reviewing projections, holding production meetings, making sales calls—right back in the rat race again. All I had done was switch uniforms. Everything else— the people, the problems, the aggravation—was pretty much the same."

Never had a chance meeting with a stranger made such an impact on my thinking, though I finally concluded that Dan's situation was not unique. Consciously or not, Dan had developed a true purpose to his life, something that he both enjoyed and apparently was quite good at. But what started it all was when he took bold action—so bold that it shocked everyone who knew and worked with him—by giving up his lofty position in the fast lane of the brokerage business. I use the adjective *bold* because it takes *bold* action to overcome the mental gravitational pull of homeostasis.

Then, when he started out making stained-glass windows in his garage, it was his second proactive move. He was in control, and happiness followed as a natural result. But as he allowed events to take control of his destiny, he became reactive and made decisions that were not in sync with what he had discovered made him happy. Finally, when his business operation became too big, he no longer enjoyed his work. As he said, he didn't realize what he had lost until it was too late.

Meaninglessness

Based on his narration, my feeling is that Dan missed the moral of his own story. He had been searching for years for the bliss he had felt at that magical moment on his front steps, yet the events leading up to that moment indicated no conscious search for it on his part. Rather, he just seemed to be naturally relaxed and enjoying his work. It sounded as though he had experienced Aristotle's description of happiness as a condition rather than a destination.

Viktor Frankl described this phenomenon as the concept of "paradoxical intention," explaining that "Happiness . . . cannot be pursued . . . [T]he more we aim at it, the more we miss our aim." If there is a reason for happiness, happiness ensues. It is a side effect of having a purpose, a meaning to life.

That, I believe, is the real key to what Dan had experienced but could never seem to get back to. His happiness had ensued as a side effect of his living the kind of life he enjoyed. The temptation is to believe he was happy because he had rid himself of his drive to succeed, but I don't believe that was the case at all. I believe that, without being consciously aware of it, what Dan had found after leaving the brokerage business was a meaning to life.

For the first time, he was doing what he wanted to do, what he enjoyed doing, and what he obviously was good at. Then, again without realizing it was happening, he allowed events to take control of his life. Since then, he had been pursuing something that was nothing more than a by-product of his previously meaningful life. For fifteen years, instead of focusing on reclaiming the meaning, he had been focusing on pursuing happiness.

Again, Frankl gives us some insight when he states in *Man's Search for Meaning*, "What man needs is not a tensionless state, but rather the striving and struggling of some goal worthy of him." I fully agree with Frankl's belief that man's real purpose is not to achieve goals, but to constantly strive toward them.

Dr. Frankl's work in this area spans more than a half century. As early as the 1950s, he referred to meaninglessness as "the mass neurosis of our time" and correctly predicted a dramatic increase in the problem. Since the turbulent Sixties, young people have been lunging in every direction in search of a cause. I remember one young lady in my employ telling me that she and her husband had been professional campus protesters when they were in college. Of and by itself, that was not earth-shaking news.

What was fascinating, however, was her recalling that on several occasions, in the midst of raucous, sometimes violent, campus demonstrations, she had asked her husband, "Now, why are we doing this?" or "What's this protest about?" Like Eric Hoffer's true believers, they were desperately looking for a reason to crusade, for a worthy cause to believe in.

In other words, much of the youth revolt over the past five decades has been due to a lack of purpose in the lives of young people. All too often this lack of purpose leads to depression, which in turn leads to suicide. Regardless of whether protest marches have to do with eradicating poverty or saving whales from extinction, the reality is that they do not fill the void inherent in a meaningless life. Consider that if man were to succeed in ridding the world of all disease, poverty, pestilence, famine, and war, what, then, would be the purpose of his existence?

The reality is that as the struggle for day-to-day survival has increasingly subsided, an important question has emerged: Survival for what? In other words, just having the means to live is not enough; a person must have something to live *for*. If there is no purpose to an individual's life—no meaning—then there's no reason to get out of bed in the morning, no reason to be alive. In the words of the great Albert Einstein, "The man who regards his life as meaningless is not merely unhappy but hardly fit for life."

The term *meaning to life* can be defined in a variety of ways by different people. For purposes of this book, however, I am referring only to meaning that has to do with career or occupational goals and normal, day-to-day living. Specifically, I am not addressing spiritual meaning, i.e., meaning that has to do with the ultimate purpose of life, a higher meaning than our life here on Earth.

The Fantasy that Never Arrives

The more I reflect on the question, and the more I draw from my own experience and the experiences of others, the more convinced I am that striving toward goals is not a means to an end, but, rather, an end in itself. Those who wish their lives away in anticipation of achieving some long-awaited goal do themselves a grave disservice. Often, it isn't even a specific goal they are seeking. Instead, they embody the future in the shadowy allure of some undefinable promised land down the road. Promised lands, however, are hard to come by.

Perhaps you've read the fascinating essay "The Station," in which the author metaphorically describes all of us as being on a mythical train of life, rolling relentless down the tracks toward the future. As we travel on this train of life, we keep believing that just around the next bend we're going to arrive at the Station, a beautiful little red station house that will signify the panacea moment when all the pieces of our lives will fit together like completed jigsaw puzzles. When we arrive at the Station, there will be a big crowd cheering, flags will be waving, bands will be playing, and that's when all our goals will be achieved and all our desires fulfilled.

Unfortunately, there's one problem with all this: It's a fantasy—a pure fantasy—because there is no station. It doesn't exist. And if there is no station, you had better enjoy the trip down the tracks. The truth is that *the* moment never quite arrives. There's always one more deal to close, one more goal to achieve, one more hill to climb—which is why you have to live in the present. The best day really is today. Forget about today being the first day of the rest of your life. Today could be the *last* day of the rest of your life. Remember, you cannot change the inevitable, but you *can* change your attitude toward today. It *is* within your power to cultivate the habit of living in the present.

Voltaire gave us wise advice when he cautioned, "Do not anxiously expect what has not yet come. Do not vainly regret what has already past." An unknown author put it much simpler when he said, "Yesterday is a cancelled check; tomorrow is a promissory note; but today is cash."

No one ever said on his deathbed, "Gee, I wish I had spent more time thinking about the future." The future doesn't need your attention. It has an annoying habit of arriving ahead of schedule—without your help. Even if you have goals, day-to-day life has little meaning if your main reason for living is just to look forward to the day when those goals are achieved. It's possible to achieve all your goals in life, but miss out on life itself. And to live life—to live in the present—one must have a meaning to his daily life.

This thought struck me more than three decades ago when I was watching a television interview of Chuck Noll, then coach of the Pittsburgh Steelers, after his team had won an unprecedented fourth Super Bowl. The interviewer, undoubtedly expecting a classic jock reply, must have been quite surprised when Noll said, "You know, I really don't get that excited about winning the Super Bowl. What excites me is working *toward* the Super Bowl—the daily practices, teaching the intricacies of blocking and tackling, the day-to-day camaraderie among the players—but the Super Bowl itself is sort of anticlimactic."

What Chuck Noll clearly was saying was that he lives life each and every day, not just for the future attainment of a Super Bowl victory. It reminded me of the late Andy Rooney's advice about learning to enjoy the little things in life, because the big ones don't come around very often. If he's lucky, an NFL coach or player may play in a Super Bowl once or twice in his career—but he has to practice every day.

Present Living Questions

Over a period of many years, I constructed a list of simple questions that I believe need to be answered by anyone who is serious about fostering the Present Living Habit. Your answers to these five questions are critical to your ability to live in the present, as well to your chances of achieving long-term, positive results, so I urge you to give them a lot of thought before attempting to set specific goals. Otherwise, you may wake up one day and realize that you've wasted many years of your life trying to achieve goals that weren't in harmony with who and what you really are.

Question No. 1: What Do I Enjoy?

To avoid the temptation to wish away precious time in anticipation of the day when a particular goal is achieved requires, first and foremost, the capacity to enjoy the struggle along the way. In other words, striving must be an end in itself.

Sadly, most people are unhappy in their work. How many happy stewardesses, waiters, bank tellers, or postal workers do you run into in a week's time? Listening to people talk, it seems as though they believe that if they could just make more money, they would enjoy their work. But I think it's the other way around, i.e., if they enjoyed their work more, they probably would make more money.

It's very easy to fool yourself on this one. If you get all steamed up and say to yourself, "Okay, I'm really going to get enthused about my work, because I want to see if it produces financial results," it probably won't. You have to genuinely enjoy what you do; work should be an end in itself. As with happiness, the more you make money your aim, the less likely you are to hit your target.

The secret is to figure out what you enjoy doing, without regard to money. No one can predict what the financial rewards ultimately might be if you possess a great enough love for your work. Can you imagine Walt Disney trying to convince bankers that he could build an empire based on a mouse? Or how about Ray Kroc? To most people, a hamburger stand is a hamburger stand, but to Kroc it was a passion that evolved into a multibillion-dollar hamburger-stand empire.

Charles A. Garfield, president of Peak Performance Center in Berkeley, California, has studied successful people for many years in an attempt to identify common characteristics of high achievers. One of the more interesting things he has found is that super-successful people avoid falling into the "comfort zone," a term he coined to describe that no man's land where a person begins to feel too much at home after experiencing a little success.

I am convinced that it's the joy of work—loving what one does for a living—that makes it not only possible to avoid the comfort zone, but easy. What else keeps tycoons like Warren Buffet, Kirk Kerkorian, and other elderly successes driving themselves relentlessly day after day? People such as Buffet and Kerkorian, who are nearing the century mark, have found "a game worth playing"—a game they *enjoy.* Remember, it's not chronology that is the essence of life; it's aliveness. To paraphrase George Burns, *getting* older may be inevitable, but *being* old isn't.

I recall reading a fascinating article some years back about the late Edward DeBartolo, the then eighty-year-old shopping-center magnate from Youngstown, Ohio. According to the article, DeBartolo worked seven days a week, getting to work every morning at 5 a.m. But that was mild compared to this: Edward DeBartolo claimed he had never taken a vacation! I happened to mention this to one of my children who was still languishing in the Age of Infinite Wisdom, and he replied, "What's the sense of being so rich if you can't enjoy it?" To which I responded, "Who said Mr. DeBartolo doesn't enjoy life? Maybe he's on vacation seven days a week. Maybe he just loves what he's doing."

Clearly, it's not the goals they reach or the amount of money they accumulate that makes financial heavyweights like Buffet, Kerkorian, and DeBartolo continue to play every point as though it were match point. It's the game that's important to them; it's the game that makes life worth living. The game is here and now; it's the present; it gives life its meaning. The real challenge is to find the right game, a game worth playing. And of utmost importance in finding a game worth playing is to find a game you enjoy.

Which leads to the next question:

Question No. 2: What Am I Good At?

The nice thing about this question is that the answer to it is often the very thing that you most enjoy. We're continually told about studies that show that the average person uses only a small percentage of his potential. I believe that at least one of the reasons for this is that most people do not exploit their best talents. You have to have a clear understanding of both your abilities and your deficiencies in order to determine how to make the most of your natural resources.

In this regard, it's important to understand that it's not what you *have* or what you *do*, but what you *do* with what you *have*. I certainly could never run the 100-yard dash in ten seconds flat, no matter how much I practiced, but that doesn't prevent me from succeeding in other fields of endeavor where I'm much better qualified. However, if I delude myself about my abilities, I'm destined to fail. Wouldn't most of us love to be Tom Brady? But just because we would enjoy being a superstar pro quarterback doesn't mean we have the ability to be one.

What I'm talking about here is maximizing your talents and efficiently using your natural resources. You have to analyze your skills with complete objectivity, which requires that you be neither modest nor egotistical. Are you creative? Athletic? Artistic? Do you like people? Are you good with numbers? Do you thrive on being organized? Are you an effective motivator? Are you skilled at orchestrating a project or better at following through on the details? The list of questions is as long as you want to make it, and you can't make it too long.

Mannequin Atrocities

In my early twenties, I spent two years in dental school, though I was never quite sure why I was there. I had given no thought whatsoever to my skills and deficiencies, ignoring the fact that kids used to call me Superclaw in art class in high school.

In dental school, you work on artificial mouths mounted on metal poles—sort of like stripped-down mannequins. Things got so bad that I became the only dental student in history to make a mannequin scream. I'll never forget the day I finally quit dental school, because as I walked out the laboratory door for the last time, I could hear all the mannequins in the laboratory cheering in unison. Talk about getting no respect.

My point is that people often stumble or get trapped into careers without giving much thought to their talents, without even considering the possibility that they may only be exploiting a small percentage of their potential in their present occupation. I sometimes think we're just too close to ourselves to see the obvious. Because it's so easy to miss your own talents, be sure to give this one a lot of attention and objectively think about what your greatest strengths are. The chances are overwhelming that efficient utilization of those strengths will also give you the most enjoyment, which will save you from being obsessed with making money. The money will come as a natural consequence, but you won't have to think about it. You'll be too busy enjoying your work and living in the present.

Question No. 3: What Do I Want Out of Life?

When I talk about the question "What do I want out of life?" I'm not referring to specific goals. Goal-setting is important, not only to assure that you keep moving forward, but also as a means of checking your progress. However, it's only after you've determined the answers to the five Present Living Questions that you're in a position to set specific goals.

Beware the Mad-Hatter Syndrome: So many people seem as though they're in a terrible hurry to get somewhere in life, but when you talk to them, it's obvious they don't have the vaguest notion where they're going. It's as though they believe that expending energy is a satisfactory substitute for reason. As my late friend Zig Ziglar used to caution, you have to be careful not to become a "wandering generality;" you must strive to become a "meaningful specific." How can you draw to yourself the things, people, and circumstances needed to transform your desires into physical realities if you don't know what it is you're after?

What I'm referring to here is a general concept of what you want out of life, a kind of overall objective that becomes your foundation for the ongoing process of setting specific goals. Take the life of Will Durant, for example. Durant spent more than seventy years traveling the world and studying the history of civilizations to write his eleven-volume series on the subject. Each of the massive volumes that Durant wrote undoubtedly served as goals or benchmarks along the way, and he probably achieved thousands of sub-goals within each volume.

However, his day-to-day study of civilizations must certainly have been an end in itself, i.e., the activity that gave purpose and meaning to his life. In other words, his daily studying and writing about civilizations must have given him a feeling of ongoing fulfillment that was far greater than the accomplishment of finally finishing his seventy years of work.

The reason the first Present Living Question (What do I enjoy?) is so important is because the person who claims to want something, but doesn't know why he wants it, is most probably headed in the wrong direction. It's very important to know *why* you want something, because it's the *why* that gives you the desire needed to persevere during tough times. And regardless of your occupation, you *will* experience tough times. In addition, you should be able to verbalize, quickly and simply, precisely what your purpose is. If you're not able to do so, the chances are good that you aren't really serious about your purpose in life.

Unfortunately, I believe that the main objective of most people, consciously or unconsciously, is simply "to make a lot of money" (whatever that's supposed to mean). A majority of people cling to the notion that making a lot of money would make them happy. But, sadly, they delude themselves. The will to money is just another form of the will to power, and the will to power always brings about self-destruction.

Much like sexual overactivity, it is really nothing more than an escape. The more a person seeks sexual pleasure just for the sake of proving his sexuality, the more he fails to find pleasure and the more miserable he is. Again, the same is true when money becomes an end in itself. Instead of possessing money, what happens when an individual's goal is money is that he becomes possessed by money. I don't think it's possible for someone to embrace the Present Living Habit if his goal is just to make a lot of money.

I believe that what each of us really wants is happiness, and to the extent we aspire to riches, it's only because we erroneously believe that money will make us happy. Remember, happiness is a by-product of a meaningful life. And, as millions of people have discovered, making money, of and by itself, does not make for a meaningful life. That is not to say you can't be happy with money, and it's not to say that money can't buy you many things that can make your life more pleasant. But, like happiness, money must be a side effect of a higher purpose.

Further, you must stay focused on your main purpose or you can inadvertently dissipate valuable energy by trying to grab all the candy in the store. Diluting your focus is a major but common mistake, and in this regard we would all be wise to heed General Patton's emphasis on the importance of singleness of purpose. I've seen this mistake made time and again, including by yours truly.

Ironically, one of the things that causes a person to lose his focus is success itself. Making large sums of money can disorient you if you don't keep reminding yourself what your chief aim in life is. The problem, I believe, stems from money's tendency to give us a false sense of omnipotence. Richard Bach makes this point poetically in *The Bridge Across Forever* when he warns, "To be handed a lot of money is to be handed a glass sword, blade-first. Best handle it very carefully, sir, very slowly while you puzzle what it's for."

The Publishing Asylum

In 1980, after having authored three bestselling books, I became restless and started looking for a side occupation. (Note: The most successful people in history rarely, if ever, have had side occupations. Hobbies, yes, but not occupations. Laser-like focus is perhaps the most common trademark of the super-successful.) I rationalized that since I had published the hardcover editions of my own books and successfully marketed them, it would make sense to publish other authors' books as well.

I had the misfortune of hitting one out of the park with the very first book I published, which is analogous to going to Las Vegas for the first time and coming away a winner. The book was a doom-and-gloom treatise on investing called *Crisis Investing*, which had already been published by a small publisher and had peaked out at about ten thousand copies. I felt the book had merit, and with what Jimmy Carter had done to the economy, along with the always destructive actions of the U.S. Congress, it seemed a perfect time to capitalize on the public's concerns.

The problem, however, was trying to convince the hardcover publisher who had distributed my own books to promote *Crisis Investing* to its retail accounts. At my urging, the vice president with whom I worked at that company read the book, after which he offered the opinion that it was a piece of (expletive). He then had his sales force review the book, and told me that the prevailing opinion was that it would be lucky to sell five thousand copies without a big marketing push—perhaps twenty-five thousand copies with a "super-duper Ringer ad campaign."

Notwithstanding all this negativism, I managed to prevail and succeeded in getting the book distributed nationwide. I wrote all the copy for nationwide ad campaign, and, to everyone's amazement, sales of the book immediately went through the ceiling. Even more amazing, *Crisis Investing* ultimately enjoyed a string of fifteen straight weeks in the number-one position on the *New York Times* bestseller list and became the biggest-selling hardcover book of 1980.

It was wildly exciting at first, but when I started to comprehend what it all meant, it made me a bit uneasy. Something just didn't feel right. As I've said many times over the years, in retrospect I wish I would have failed with that first book, because that would have ended my foray into the book publishing business.

Instead, I forged ahead with a number of other books, marketing them in the same sensationalistic style I had used to promote *Crisis Investing*. To my astonishment, less than nine months after publishing *Crisis Investing*, the *Wall Street Journal* ran a front-page story on my publishing exploits, and *Fortune* soon countered with a three-page article, noting that I had managed to get three books on the *New York Times* bestseller list after less than a year in business.

I vividly recall feeling genuinely embarrassed when I read the articles, and I assure you it had nothing to do with modesty.

Rather, it was because I knew in my heart that the articles were premature. **Real-World Rule No. 87: No matter how great others tell you you are, if you don't feel good about what you're doing, ignore the applause, stop, and carefully evaluate the facts.**

The truth of the matter was that I knew all along—at least subconsciously—what was wrong. I not only was publishing many books I didn't really believe in, I also was saying things in my ads that were beyond the bounds of acceptable marketing hype. Talk about not being able to look in the mirror; I had to shave in a dark closet. I was guilty of self-delusion as a result of fearing the truth, which is an easy trap to fall into when you start seeing money as an end in itself.

The one good thing that came out of all this was that it gave me a firsthand appreciation of what conventional publishers have to put up with in dealing with authors. They are constantly being chastised for being insensitive and calloused toward no-name authors, especially first-time authors.

However, based on my experience from inside the publishing asylum, I can tell you that there are most decidedly two sides to the story. If man does, indeed, walk around in a state of waking dreams, most would-be authors float around in a self-hypnotic state of delusions that defies description. The one thing that most unpublished authors have in common is that they believe, in their heart of hearts, that they've written the sequel to *Gone With the Wind*—or at least *Think and Grow Rich*—and they make demands accordingly.

On more than one occasion, I had to control myself from laughing out loud when dealing with these wannabe authors, but would quickly remind myself that the author with whom I was speaking might very well be dangerous. Who knew what these people were capable of when they were running around loose on the streets? It got to a point where my staff and I would spend a large percentage of our time discussing strategies to humor some of our most deranged authors. When I finally extricated myself from the publishing business, I could have written a great movie script based on my zany experiences. I can just see myself accepting my Oscar for *Psycho Author.*

The moral? I didn't have a good reason for going into the publishing business. Certainly, I didn't enjoy it and, other than writing good ad copy, I had no particular skills for running a publishing company. The best guide to a proper focus is to think about what would bring happiness to your daily life. What is it you really enjoy, that you're good at, that would make life worth living? What is it that you really want out of life, that would make living in the present an easy habit to practice?

Question No. 4: What's the price?

One of the realities of life is that we all have endless desires, but very limited time. Therefore, what we want out of life isn't the only issue. The price of what we want has to be figured into the equation. This should not be viewed as a negative, because if everything in life were easy—if success came without a price tag—it would be hard to appreciate anything. For example, what gives life itself such a high value is death, which is why we are willing to pay almost any price necessary to stay alive. There are many things we would like to do, but because we know they would endanger or shorten our lives, we refrain from doing them.

When considering what you want out of life, you have to give the price serious consideration. The price can present itself in many forms, such as time, energy, pain, and/or sacrifice. Because of the Natural Law of Balance, sacrifice is an inescapable price. Remember, there is always is an offsetting negative to every positive situation. Your foremost desire in life may conflict with many other things you want, and sacrificing those other things could be a significant part of the cost. For example, you may have to sacrifice recreation, relaxation, and/or time with your family.

Also, human nature being what it is, the price of success usually includes having to endure the jealousy and resentment of others. It can get pretty ugly at times, often draining you of limited supplies of time and energy. Some people have difficulty handling this kind of discomfort, so it's another reality that should be addressed in advance.

Which leads to the final question:

Question No. 5: Am I Willing to Pay the Price?

This is the easiest of the questions to fool yourself on, because it's so easy to say *yes*. But a serious *yes* means you're prepared to be totally dedicated to the pursuit you've chosen. You should be so committed to your purpose that you develop what Napoleon Hill referred to as "a white heat of desire."

Unfortunately, we can never know for certain how big the price is, or whether we're willing to pay it, until we're actually tested. In other words, the best we can do is believe that we're willing to pay the price, but it's up to events to prove us right or wrong. This, however, should not prevent you from making the best possible evaluation of your willingness ahead of time. Certainly, if you have doubts about the price in advance, the chances are pretty good that you'll bail out at the first sign of trouble.

Thus, seeking a meaningful purpose to your life can be a tricky proposition. You may want something badly, but not badly enough to pay the necessary price. As I said earlier, this is why it's so important to know *why* you want something. It's the why that gives you the desire that in turn makes you willing to pay the price.

Serious Business

When I was much younger, I felt that questions concerning goals and purpose in life were elementary at best. I held firmly to this belief until well past the time I graduated from the Age of Infinite Wisdom phase of my life. However, the more real-life experience I've accumulated, the more I've come to realize just how important goals and purpose are. As a result, I take very seriously the five

Present Living Questions that I've discussed in this chapter, and I urge you to do the same. Making money is not that difficult once you've laid the proper foundation, but I'm convinced that it's the foundation where most people fall short.

That said, because I know all too well just how easy it is to become cavalier when it comes to studying the five Present Living Questions, I'd like to offer some suggestions on how to go about answering them.

First, force yourself to write down both the questions and answers because it forces you to be clear. One of the most important rules a writer learns early in his career is that unclear writing is a sign of unclear thinking.

Second, to the extent possible, you should do your thinking in a quiet, secluded place. Over the years, I've spent hundreds of hours looking out over the ocean and pondering the Present Living Questions.

Third, take all the time you need to think through both the questions and your answers. It's imperative that you not rush your answers, because it takes time to make certain that you aren't kidding yourself.

Fourth, avoid discussing these questions with friends or relatives. It's not that they aren't well-meaning; on the contrary, they usually are. It's just that the more you discuss them with other people, the less likely it is that the answers will be yours.

Finally, never forget that the one absolutely certain thing about life is that circumstances continually change, so periodically step back and review your progress, and if you don't seem to be getting to where you want to be in life, reevaluate your answers. This is perhaps the most important point of all, because, as human beings, we are in a continual state of change. This causes our priorities to change, too, often without our being consciously aware of it.

For example, a person may at one point in his life be unwilling to pay the price of traveling and being away from his family several days a week. But when his children reach their teen years, that may no longer be a major consideration. (In fact, he may jump at the chance to get away from his teenage children.)

In my case, I remember when making money was my main objective, but making money as an end in itself long ago dropped off my list of priorities. Why? Because I learned that money, like happiness, is but a side effect of pursuing a meaning in life. To the extent one has a purposeful life, making money becomes a rather easy proposition.

This is such an important principle that it's impossible to overemphasize it. If I can save just one reader the wasted time, energy, and attendant unhappiness that result from being imprisoned by the will to money, the repetition is worth it. Do not allow yourself to get caught in the insidious money trap. It's a lot harder to get out than it is to get in.

The Bonus

Lastly, one of the nice bonuses to having a meaningful purpose in life, and in turn being able to live in the present, is something I refer to as the Positive Life Cycle. As with the habits that bring it about, the essence of the Positive Life Cycle is quite simple:

The more certain you are about your purpose in life, the more focused you'll be on living in the present and the more enthusiastic you'll be in your day-to-day work; the more you display the Present Living Habit and enthusiasm in your daily work, the more likely you are to attract the attention of positive, enthusiastic people; the more positive, enthusiastic people you attract, the more successful you'll be; and the more successful you are, the more present-living oriented and enthusiastic you'll be.

Thus, what you set in motion when your life has the kind of meaning that promotes the Present Living Habit is a self-perpetuating cycle of enthusiasm and success. This cycle, in turn, adds fuel to the dynamic mental process that draws to you the things, people, and circumstances needed to translate the mental image of what you want out of life into physical reality.

CHAPTER 5

THE MORALITY HABIT

One of the earmarks of a civilization is a generally accepted moral code, or standard of behavior, upon which most of its laws are based. Ideally, I agree with the philosophy that every individual should have the right to take whatever action he chooses, so long as he does not forcibly interfere with the rights of others. In the real world, however, idealism is fantasy.

The reason there is a perceived need for laws is that there is widespread disagreement as to when the actions of one individual interferes with the rights of others. For example, if there was no generally accepted code of conduct (i.e., if we lived in a totally free society), a person would have the right to walk down the street with no clothes on. Such an individual could argue that he is neither committing aggression against anyone nor trying to convert others to his way of thinking, so he should be allowed to do as he pleases. However, most people would disagree with this viewpoint and insist that such behavior does infringe on their rights. They might justifiably argue that they are, in essence, being forced to view something that they deem to be obscene or, at the very least, unpleasant. The operative word here is *forced*.

I bring up this philosophical point because it presents a fundamental problem when it comes to consistency in your day-to-day conduct. There are probably a great many morally based laws on the books with which you disagree. By the same token, there are actions that are technically legal that you may believe should be outlawed on moral grounds. A tough question to tackle, then, is whether or not you should obey laws that you feel are immoral.

It's important to constantly remind yourself that you are not operating in an antiseptic laboratory stocked with rational people brimming over with rational thoughts. If you ignore this reality, you do so at your own peril. For example, man-made laws are a reality, regardless of whether or not they are rational or moral, and regardless of whether or not you or I like them. Therefore, within reason, and to the extent possible, you should attempt to obey man-made laws, if only because it is pragmatic to do so. It's extremely difficult to achieve any great amount of success operating from a prison cell.

With these prefacing remarks as a caveat, I now want to emphasize the other side of the morality coin: Though you may choose to obey certain laws for pragmatic reasons, that should have little or no effect on your personal moral beliefs. On the contrary, an important key to success is to clearly define your own set of moral standards as a guide to your daily behavior, while not losing sight of the realities of man-made laws. Put another way, you should be honest because you want to, not because you have to.

The Necessity for Clear Values

Defining your moral standards serves as an ethical compass that prevents you from straying off course when the winds of temptation begin howling around your ship of life. Millions of people continually crash on the rocks of bad consequences, often suffering irreparable damage because they allowed themselves to get trapped in rough waters without first making sure they had their ethical compasses aboard.

It's imperative to understand that for any strategy or plan of action to be sound, it must begin with a solid moral foundation. Without such a foundation, anything a person tries to build is destined to crumble. The bad effect of a bad cause may not show up immediately, but you can be certain that ultimately it will make its appearance. When I speak of establishing a strong moral foundation, I'm talking about possessing a clear set of values that predetermines your day-to-day behavior. You need to know what you believe in ahead of time in order to understand why you should do things a certain way. What do you believe is moral? What do you believe is immoral? What do you believe is ethical? What do you believe is unethical? What do you believe is good? What do you believe is evil?

If you don't formulate your moral beliefs ahead of time, your actions may inadvertently be based on spur-of-the-moment whims, on emotion, on instant gratification. In other words, you're likely to revise your ethical standards to fit each new situation as it arises, a practice commonly referred to as "situational ethics." An individual who engages in situational ethics is someone who does not possess a fixed standard of right and wrong. Right is simply whatever he perceives to be in his immediate best interest at any given time, which is a fool-proof formula for failure. It's imperative that you decide on a clear, concise set of moral values when your intellect is in control. Then, in highly emotional situations, you're more likely to act in accordance with the moral standards that you have decided—in advance—to live by.

The Overriding Issue

In this chapter, I purposely do not address morality as it relates to areas such as drugs, pornography, and abortion. These are hot topics for debate, and in a large percentage of cases they are tied to the spiritual beliefs of the debaters. However, such topics are beyond the scope of this book, and hundreds, if not thousands, of books have been written on each of them.

In my view, the key moral issue that needs to be addressed for purposes of this book is honesty. Plain and simple, honesty is the absolute refusal to lie, steal, cheat, or deceive in any way. Admittedly, that's a pretty rigid definition. Does it mean that we're all dishonest? Yes, because, as human beings, we're all imperfect. Actually, it would be more proper to say that each of us defines *lie, steal, cheat,* and *deceive* in our own way.

I acknowledge that what follows constitutes my own subjective views regarding honesty, and I offer these views only as food for thought. In the final analysis, however, you must formulate your own guidelines regarding honesty in order to acquire the Morality Habit in a meaningful way. What's most important is that you do your formulating in advance, before being confronted with a situation that appeals to your instant-gratification instincts.

The terms *lie, steal, cheat,* and *deceive* tend to overlap, so in discussing honesty I won't attempt to distinguish between them. For brevity's sake, I'll focus most of my comments on the subject of lying, but keep in mind that when one lies, one is often equally guilty of stealing, cheating, and deceiving, as well.

Also, I have made no attempt to address such areas as "The Big Lie," compulsive lying, premeditated lying, or malevolent lying. I am assuming that your intentions are good and that you are basically honest. The person with bad intentions—who *intends* to act dishonestly—has a whole different set of problems that are outside the focus of this book. Good intentions are a given; however, good intentions are not enough. To win in the real world, sound moral practices must be *implemented* through force of habit.

The Little White Lie

All of us tell what are commonly known as little white lies, or what I like to refer to as "convenience lies." A person would have to possess a severe case of self-righteousness syndrome in order to believe he is never guilty of telling little white lies. For example, when you tell your secretary to tell Mr. Smith that you're not in, but you're at your desk, the reality is that you're lying. Someone may want to challenge me on this point and insist that I'm being too technical, that something so insignificant shouldn't be considered a lie. Perhaps, but let's examine it more closely and see:

"Were you in your office when Mr. Smith called?"

"Yes."

"Were you sitting at your desk?"

"Yes."

"Did you tell your secretary to tell Mr. Smith you weren't in?"

"Yes."

"Was your statement true or false?"

Many people might be inclined to answer, "Technically, it was false, but I wasn't lying."

Talk about self-delusion, the reality is that a knowingly false statement is a lie, no matter how insignificant it may be in your eyes.

Real-World Rule No. 274: The problem with little white lies is that they tend to lead to bigger and bigger lies, which in turn lead to more and more bad consequences.

The Exaggeration Lie

Another common form of lying that most people don't normally think of as lying is exaggeration. Nothing makes me lose confidence in a person more quickly than to discover he's inflated his facts or feats.

One must be ever vigilant when it comes to exaggeration lies, because, as with little white lies, they often wear an ever-so-subtle mask. For example, a little thing like leaving so-called urgent messages for people is usually an exaggeration lie. To my way of thinking, the word *urgent* implies something close to a life-or-death matter. If the message really isn't urgent, then the person who leaves such a message sustains a substantial loss of credibility. The same is true when you tell someone that if he'll meet with you, you'll only take five minutes of his time, then you end up taking thirty minutes. As a result, you gain a well-deserved reputation as the little boy who cries wolf and you don't get in the door again.

The $100,000-A-Year Salesman

Say that a real estate salesman tells you he made "about $100,000" last year. (Did you ever notice that all real estate salespeople made "about $100,000" last year—never $50,000 or $75,000, but always "about $100,000?") On closer scrutiny, however, you find that the figure wasn't quite $100,000. It was actually $88,000, but the salesman conveniently rounded it off on the high side—and even that figure represented his *gross* commissions! Further, since most sales commissions are split with another brokerage firm, that left him with only about $44,000. And if he's a salesman, the broker who employs him got roughly half of the $44,000 as his cut, which left the salesman with only $22,000.

But there's still a little something called "overhead" to be figured in. (You know what overhead is: that mysterious cost phenomenon that is unique only to your business. No one else has overhead, right?) So, by the time the $100,000-a-year salesman deducts incidentals such as gas, auto maintenance, supplies, treating prospects to lunch and dinner, and various other miscellaneous expenses, what he really netted was a grand total of $8,422.87—quite a comedown from $100,000!

This year, of course, things aren't going nearly as well for him, so if you follow this $100,000-a-year salesman home some fine evening, don't be surprised to find that he's moved from his sparsely furnished studio apartment into a medium-sized tent. The truth is that it's a semantic error to refer to his "about $100,000 last year" statement as an exaggeration, because it evades the real issue—that it's an exaggeration *lie.*

A good formula for reducing inflated income claims down to realistic size is to be found in **Real-World Rule No. 288: When someone tries to impress you with a boxcar-sized income, divide his figure by two, then multiply by one, divide by three, and circle the subtotal in red. After that, wad the paper up in a ball, throw it against the wall, jump up and down on it four times, then straighten it out again and put it on the table. Finally, add three, subtract eight, multiply by two, and divide by five. Then, just to be on the safe side, subtract another seven. As simple as that, you've got the guy's real income.**

A Free Shine

A final example of the exaggeration lie that stands out in my mind occurred when I was in New Orleans to speak at a hard-money financial conference. The evening I was scheduled to speak, I was still in my bathrobe in my hotel suite, preparing to shave, when I heard a knock at the door. I opened it and, to my surprise, found the then-governor of California, Jerry Brown, staring me in the face. He had been brought to my room by a mutual acquaintance, Michael, who was a political animal. Michael had always been obsessed with gaining the friendship of politicians (remember, mental sickness can take many forms), and he himself had once made an unsuccessful bid for a congressional seat in his district.

As he walked through the door, Michael enthusiastically introduced Governor Brown to me, then bellowed, "Jerry, Robert is the guy I told you about who has a million of his newsletter readers' names on computer." It was a great intro, except for one thing: Michael and I had discussed my newsletter list on several occasions, and he knew full well that the figure was more in the area of thirty thousand names. As Governor Brown dropped to the floor and began buffing my slippers with his iridescent purple and orange tie, my instinctive urge was to correct Michael's gross overstatement. However, within a matter of a couple minutes he reemphasized the figure *one million*, so it was a very awkward situation. Besides, I liked the way the shine on my slippers was coming out.

Nonetheless, Michael's blatant exaggeration made me realize that I could never again take anything he said at face value. It didn't take any great amount of genius to figure out that he was trying to impress Jerry Brown with his connections to people who owned valuable mailing lists that could lead to something spelled *c-o-n-t-r-i-b-u-t-i-o-n-s*.

When it comes to fighting off the temptation to exaggerate, it's wise to practice the wisdom of **Real-World Rule No. 74: Always let people be surprised that you gave them more than you promised, faster than you promised, and that it was easier than you promised.** Using this rule as a guide, you'll stand out from the rest of the crowd like a thinking man at a Joe Biden rally.

The Omission Lie

Omitting relevant information is one of the most frequently employed forms of lying, and one of the most difficult to reconcile. It's tricky business because certainly you are not obligated to tell every person with whom you're involved everything about your life. The guideline I use to determine whether or not something should be omitted (i.e., whether or not I have a moral obligation to volunteer certain information) is to ask myself: Will the other party draw erroneous conclusions and thereby make decisions injurious to himself as a result of his not knowing about something I've withheld? If so, then the omission would be a lie.

Admittedly, this is a less than precise guideline, which is why lying through omission is so difficult to monitor. Often, it's in the eyes of the beholder, but what's important is to get in the habit of going out of your way *not* to omit facts. That said, the fact is that most cases of lying through omission are not borderline; they are blatant.

I recall a business deal I was involved in during the early 1970s. A business associate and I had bought a controlling interest in an American Stock Exchange company after prolonged negotiations with the major shareholders. On the surface, the company appeared to be very strong, with an 11-to-1 current ratio and about $4 million cash in the bank (about $16 million in today's dollars). In addition, sales of the company's main product line were represented on the books (and had been verbally confirmed) to be very strong.

What we were not told, however—and did not discover until long after we had purchased our shares—was that the high sales volume was misleading, because abnormally high product returns were anticipated in the coming year. (The company's products were sold to stores strictly on a consignment basis.) As a result, the company actually was in the early stages of a downturn. Soon after we became involved, it began to experience record returns far in excess of the reserves it had maintained on its books, and the results were a devastating blow to our plans.

As an aid to guard against inadvertently lying through omission, I periodically remind myself of this classic example of intentional lying through omission. Actions do have consequences, and, over the long haul, omission liars, like all other liars, suffer the consequences they deserve. The safest, simplest, day-to-day rule to follow in this area is: When in doubt, don't leave it out.

The Sort-of-True Lie
The sort-of-true lie is used most effectively by those who have honed their lying skills to a degree where they are super smooth at their craft. If an individual on this level gets caught, he can always argue that what he said was "sort of true," or that he "must have misunderstood what you were asking."

I remember a young entrepreneur, Larry, who once visited me to discuss a business proposal. By virtue of his marathon remarks throughout our meeting, it became obvious that he was still well entrenched in the Age of Infinite Wisdom period of his life. He clearly was suffering from a severe case of delusions of grandeur, telling me, among other things, his ambition to ultimately get into politics (my eyes slowly rolling toward the ceiling on cue) and "make an impact on the world." As he spoke, I thought to myself that perhaps he should begin with a somewhat less ambitious goal than impacting the whole world. Considering his credentials, stirring up the people of Buffalo seemed perhaps a more realistic objective.

During the course of our meeting, Larry reiterated a point I had heard him make to a large group of people at an earlier date—that he had recently written a self-help book in a record thirty days. This was a task, he pointed out, that had taken an enormous amount of commitment, determination, and perseverance. I certainly agreed. When I had first heard him tell the story of how he had accomplished this incredible feat, I, like the rest of his audience, had been awed. However, because I had already authored a number of books myself, I, unlike the others in attendance, was also very skeptical.

Sure enough, not long after our one-on-one meeting, a friend happened to mention the details of how Larry's book actually had been written, *exactly as he had heard it from the professional who had ghostwritten the book* for him, including the amount of money the ghostwriter had been paid for the job. What the writer had been instructed to do was distill Larry's seminar notes and put them together in book form.

When I heard this, it occurred to me that if someone ever confronted this young entrepreneur with the facts, he could always argue that he had "sort of" written the book . . . in a way, that is. Or perhaps all the people who had heard him say he had written it had just misunderstood what he really had meant by "I wrote my book in thirty days" . . . mumble, mumble, mumble . . . ad infinitum. The sort-of-true lie is part little white lie, part exaggeration lie, and part omission lie.

A person who insists on telling sort-of-true lies should at least pick his spots carefully. If he can't resist the urge to shade the truth, he should learn to be selective with regard to whom he tells his fairy tales. The problem with massaging the truth with someone like me is that I'm one of those annoying individuals who gets around too much. I know far too many people and have a Colombo-like habit of stumbling onto the facts. If you're determined to lie, it's wise to restrict your lying to people who stay in bed all day.

There's one thing the various kinds of lies I've touched upon in this chapter have in common, and that's the price you pay when you're caught. And make no mistake about it, sooner or later you will be caught, which results in the most difficult of all losses to recoup—loss of credibility. The best protection against making an exception to your moral code just to get by an uncomfortable situation is to keep reminding yourself that in the real world, actions do indeed have consequences.

Concentricity

Integrity is an impressive sounding word, one which most people use quite freely. Unfortunately, very few people really understand what the word means, and even fewer practice it. Integrity is adherence to your code of moral values. It's one thing to talk about moral values, but quite another to consistently adhere to them. Integrity gets at the very heart of the Morality Habit issue.

During a question-and-answer period at one of my seminars, a gentleman in the audience said he believed that all government spending, with the exception of expenditures for protection of citizens' lives and property, was theft, and therefore immoral. He confessed he felt guilty because he was a builder of government housing (meaning his income was derived from money extracted primarily from unwilling individuals, euphemistically referred to as "taxpayers"). It was a lucrative business for him, and he was in a quandary as to what to do. He asked me if I thought it was wrong for him to continue to profit from this kind of business.

Of course, he knew full well what the answer was, and I felt as though he was hoping I would grant him dispensation and make everything all right. First of all, I don't have the power to grant dispensations, nor does any other human being. Integrity is a highly personal matter; you embrace it for your own sake. A hundred priests, ministers, and rabbis can forgive you, but all that matters is whether or not you can forgive yourself. There's only one way to protect your integrity: You must be ever vigilant when it comes to not compromising it. There is no other method that I know of that works.

What I'm talking about here is how well you practice what you claim to believe in. What you believe in and what you say is one thing; what you do is quite another. I like to think of this consistency of belief, words, and actions as *concentricity*. Try to imagine two perfect circles, one representing what you believe in and what you say, the other representing what you actually do. When these two circles are nearly concentric—that is, when they are almost perfectly aligned—it means you're adhering to your code of moral values.

But when the two circles begin to pull apart, it indicates that your integrity is slipping. And when what you do begins to pull too far away from what you believe in and what you say, you may find yourself looking in the mirror one morning and realizing that you're beginning to dislike and disrespect yourself. At first, you may not be able to figure out why, but if your intent is to be honest, the reason will soon emerge.

Again, we're all human, which means we're imperfect, so it's simply not possible for these two circles ever to be 100 percent concentric. But that's precisely why you have to work hard at concentricity every day of your life. It's the only way you can hope to adhere to your values on a consistent basis. The temptations to allow these two circles to pull farther and farther apart are everywhere, so it takes a good deal of self-discipline to hold them together. This is particularly true when it comes to omission lies and sort-of-true lies. It's important that concentricity becomes a way of life for you—an ingrained habit, if you will.

Case-By-Case Basis

During another seminar tour I did awhile back, I found myself faced with a difficult problem. Time was running short, and in one of the cities where I was going to be speaking, we had neglected to arrange for our audio needs. Just before arriving in that city, I made a couple of quick phone calls and was referred to an individual at a local audio company. I immediately called him, but as the conversation unfolded, some of the things he was saying made me very uncomfortable.

At one point, he emphasized to me that whenever I called I should not only ask for him, but also should be sure not to talk to anyone else at the company about this particular audio job. "Hold on," I said to myself, "what's this guy trying to tell me?" I asked him, "Now, let me be sure I understand something. Are you doing this job on behalf of your company or are you doing it on your own?" Sure enough, he told me that he was doing the job on his own.

"Well, then," I pressed forward, "if you're doing it on your own, how do you decide which jobs should go to your company and which jobs you should keep for yourself?"

To which he replied, "I take it on a case-by-case basis."

By now, I was sorry I had initiated the inquiry, because I didn't like the results and there wasn't enough time to find another good audio person. Immediately, I tried to rationalize, and I almost had myself convinced that it wasn't my problem. I told myself, "Hey, all I did was call someone who had been recommended to me, ask him if he could handle my audio needs, and anything else is none of my business. It's not my job to be the moral policeman of the world."

Man does, indeed, inhabit a world of delusions. Plain and simple, what I was trying to do was "make true that which I loved," i.e., that which was convenient to my short-term needs. As the hours rolled by, I felt those two circles in my mind almost flying in opposite directions, which caused me to take a good look in the mirror. Sure enough, there he was—Richard Nixon staring back at me.

Well, maybe not quite that bad, but I sure didn't like what I saw. I thought about the matter long and hard the rest of the day, and finally had to admit that I was guilty of trying to delude myself. Standing in front of an audience and preaching the importance of having a solid moral foundation, while at the same time knowing that the person who was recording me was at that very moment engaging in a blatantly dishonest act, was at a minimum hypocritical, at worst flat-out dishonest on my part. Any way I sliced it, the reality was that I would knowingly be helping someone lie, steal, cheat, and deceive his employer.

At the eleventh hour, I managed to save my self-respect by mustering the courage to call and cancel the technician's services. You'll recall that in relating this story, I said "there wasn't enough time to find another good audio person." What I really had meant, but didn't want to admit to myself, was that it would be *difficult* to find another good audio person on such short notice. But there's a big difference between *difficult* and *impossible*. It's the ultimate rationalization, and many people manage to rationalize their way through life by continually playing this subtle, self-delusional trick on themselves.

The point is that anyone can be honest when it doesn't cause them any inconvenience or discomfort, particularly when money is involved. Your honesty is really on the line, however, when adhering to your moral beliefs can cause you serious hardship or inconvenience. That's why you have to think through your moral beliefs ahead of time and develop the habit of sticking to those beliefs. Then, when the moment of truth arrives, you won't even have to stop to think about the right thing to do.

To strengthen your concentricity, I suggest you heed **Real-World Rule No. 211: The surest way to get good results in this life, and to go to Heaven in the next life, is to live every moment as though the whole world were watching.** In other words, by living the same kind of life in private that you live when you're in the company of others, your actions will become consistent through force of habit.

Consider the Source

This brings up the sticky problem of people sometimes thinking you're dishonest, even though you don't believe you've done anything wrong. What should you do if someone falsely accuses you of an immoral action?

For starters, your frame of reference should be that it's far more important to *be* honest than to have everyone *think* you're honest. In an imperfect world, the reality is that you can neither please everyone nor get everyone to like you. Therefore, the first thing you should do is consider the source. Look at it this way: Have you ever dealt with a dishonest person? Of course you have. Second question: Have you ever had anyone admit to you that he's dishonest? Have you ever had anyone say to you, "Honesty compels me to admit that I'm dishonest"? It's never happened, right?

So what's at the root of this seeming contradiction? Well, if you consider someone to be dishonest, that same person is almost certain to think you are dishonest, because your moral standards are different from his. Worse, oftentimes your accuser doesn't even know you, which can add even more irritation to the accusation. You should never lose sight of the fact that it's not nearly as important for someone to believe you're honest as it is for *you* to believe you're honest.

Therefore, you should not allow it to get you down if you are attacked by someone whose moral standards are different from yours. Instead, I suggest you take the advice of one of the wisest men I've ever known, who once explained to me a very sound approach to handling unjust accusations. He said that if someone falsely accuses you, just look in the mirror and say to yourself: "If my hands are clean, and my cause is just, and my demands are reasonable, I have nothing to worry about." Then simply go about your business.

At the extreme, your honest actions may sometimes make others mad, particularly in situations where people want you to cooperate with them in an act that you believe to be immoral. You should never kid yourself about your honest actions being appreciated by everyone. In our world of delusions, the reality is that integrity doesn't always make a person popular, but it does give him the greatest of all assets—an asset that money can't buy—unwavering integrity, which makes a person free, and nothing can quite match freedom.

When it comes to the Morality Habit, the wise person refuses to compromise his integrity for anybody or anything. And to the extent the Morality Habit becomes ingrained in your thinking, you greatly enhance your chances for success in all areas of life.

CHAPTER 6

THE HUMAN RELATIONS HABIT

Like it or not—and many people don't—to one extent or another you have to deal with others to achieve any reasonable degree of success. This is true regardless of your station in life and no matter what your objectives are. Further, the more successful you are in getting others to cooperate with you, and the more people you can solicit as allies, the greater your chances of achieving positive results. It can sometimes get very lonely and brutal in the Malevolent Jungle when those wild herds of humanoids start stampeding your homestead.

The issue of good human relations is pretty simple. To the extent you relate poorly to others, you tend to have a problem-filled life and success comes hard, if at all. To the extent you relate well to others, you tend to have a pleasant life, and success comes relatively easy. An individual can be brilliant at many things, yet be totally ignorant when it comes to getting along with, and gaining the cooperation of, others. Everyone knows someone who is knowledgeable about a wide variety of subjects, but seemingly has zero knowledge of human relations. In most cases, it's because the otherwise knowledgeable individual has not taken the trouble to study human relations or even given them much thought.

That's unfortunate, because, like all other habits, superior human relations is an art that anyone can learn. Some people may be born with more natural talent in this area than others, but that's true of virtually everything in life. More important is the fact that anyone can become better through practice.

At least two major pluses accrue to your benefit when you become adept at relating well to others:

First, by understanding the techniques involved in successful human relations, you attract others who appreciate these same techniques. If you make it a habit to practice those things that make you an attractive human being, you will appeal to other attractive human beings, and attractive human beings add value to your life.

Second, when you're strong in the area of human relations, you gain the cooperation of others, and this cooperation is the shortest distance between you and your goals. It's the flip side of a friction-filled life. When too many people are pulling against you, rooting against you, and begrudging your success, it's like coming up against a tsunami of roadblocks. Remember, actions have consequences, so if you treat people in negative ways, they will act negatively toward you; if you treat people in positive ways, they will act positively toward you. If that sounds simple, it's because it is. In fact, it's one of the simplest known methods for getting results, which is why it's remarkable that so few people make the effort to develop good human relations.

I should note here that many self-development authors make the mistake of urging readers to display qualities like self-esteem in their relations with others. However, as with a positive mental attitude, self-esteem cannot be willed. When someone says, "You should display self-esteem," he really is saying, "You should *fake* self-esteem." In point of fact, a quality like self-esteem is a *result* of practicing good human relations. Likewise, feelings toward you that emanate from others—such as love and respect—cannot be willed. They, too, are a result of successful human relations.

When you master the Human Relations Habit, it leads to a triple win: You make others feel better; you feel better; and, directly or indirectly, your goodwill toward others will almost certainly come back to you with interest somewhere down the road.

Keys to the Cooperation Vault

Many of the qualities and actions that lead to superior human relations are inextricably tied to effective communication. The longer I live, the more I see life as an ongoing series of miscommunications between human beings. For example, no matter how much concern you may feel for another person, you still have to communicate that concern to him. Keep in mind that in order to achieve successful human relations, you must be successful in communicating qualities such as the ones I discuss in this chapter. To merely philosophize about them is insufficient; they must be implemented, through both words and actions.

Following are some of the more important traits that I believe must become habits if one is to gain the cooperation and goodwill of others. The list is by no means complete, but more than extensive enough for our purposes. To one extent or another, you likely are already familiar with each of the traits on the list, which is good, because, in many respects, learning is just a matter of finding out what you already know. My primary objective in discussing these traits is to motivate you to move your performance in the area of human relations up a notch, or perhaps several notches.

Brevity

Nothing embarrasses me more than when I leave a meeting feeling I've overdramatized my points by being childishly redundant. People tend to be skeptical about "the lady who protests too much." We would all do well to remember the words of David Ogilvy:

"When a company boasts about its integrity, or a woman about her virtue, avoid the former and cultivate the latter." Busy people are impatient, so when you have something to say, be succinct, keep it simple, say exactly what you mean—then stop.

In both your personal and business dealings, it's wise to heed **Real-World Rule No. 148: The power of the understatement is enormous.** That which is well said is quickly said. If it's something positive, it will be that much better received if presented in a brief manner. If it's a negative, it will be less painful if it isn't dragged out. Just as unclear writing is a sign of unclear thinking, verbal rambling is a sign of not having your thoughts well organized.

Brevity is particularly vital when it comes to making business proposals. People get uneasy if they can't understand what you're talking about, so learn to stick to the facts. When you make a presentation, there are only three relevant issues that need to be addressed:

1. What, specifically, do you want from me?

2. If I give you exactly what you want, what specifically do you expect to accomplish with it?

3. If you accomplish everything you hope to, specifically, what's in it for me and what's in it for you?

Experience has taught me that when you're dealing with successful people, almost everything else you have to say beyond this is fluff. This is especially true when you're trying to raise money. Avoid being superfluous, and don't waste time on side comments designed to patronize or butter up the other party. The chances are good that he didn't acquire money to invest in the first place without being pretty sharp, so don't try to be cute with him. Always remember the advice contained in **Real-World Rule No. 267: Never try to promote a promoter.**

Compassion

While you cannot will someone to have compassion for you, you can learn to have compassion for others. Compassion involves nothing more than putting yourself in the other guy's shoes and trying to feel what he's experiencing. Unfortunately, Thoreau was right about most people living lives of quiet desperation. The average person is in pain, and if you don't take that factor into consideration before speaking or acting, you can neither help others nor gain their cooperation. To paraphrase the late Jim Rohn, you have to meet people in the hurt.

As with everything in life, you'll reap just about what you sow when it comes to compassion, and the least you can expect to gain from being compassionate is a heightened sense of self-esteem. More likely, however, you'll reap many additional rewards, both directly and indirectly, as time passes. Compassion is a common language that links together the goodwill members of the human race, helping to offset widespread negative traits such as hatred and contempt.

If it's true that every twenty-four hours the world turns over and somebody new is on top, it's also true that somebody new is on the bottom. Fortune tires of carrying anyone on her shoulders too long, and, as thousands of mega-millionaires during the past decade have found, no one is immune to financial disaster. When such disaster descends upon a Bernie Madoff type, the afflicted individual quickly discovers that there is much truth to the axiom, "Everything that goes around comes around."

In a world that operates religiously within a framework of actions and consequences, the person who demonstrates the most compassion *toward* others is the person who is destined to reap the most compassion *from* others. Making it a habit to be compassionate costs nothing, but is worth everything.

Decisiveness

I've had to work hard to nurture this habit over the years, particularly when people have tried to pressure me into committing to something that I really didn't want to do. I often used to say things like, "Let me think about it," or "Give me a call in a couple of weeks," which I now realize was very weak on my part. The result was that people would end up getting mad at me, while the guy who refused to yield to pressure and gave a flat *no* right off the bat would be long forgotten.

One day I was lamenting to a friend how I had gotten myself into a jam with someone who had made a request of me, even though I had not agreed to do what he had asked of me. My friend really opened my eyes when he said, "The reason you get into tight situations like this is that you egg people on. Instead of giving them a rigid *no* the first time they ask, you try to mumble your way out of situations and leave them up in the air. I think you're just afraid to give people a firm and final *no*."

Wow! What a revelation. After pondering my friend's point, I concluded he was absolutely right. I now recognize that it's a matter of sacrificing the short-term comfort of avoiding embarrassment, or possible negative vibrations, in exchange for long-term peace of mind—i.e., knowing that the matter has been permanently resolved. To boot, the other person ends up liking you more, not less, for having been firm with him from the outset. You didn't give him false hope (always a breeding ground for ill feelings) and didn't waste his time. In addition, you're able to completely forget about the matter and go about your business with a clear mind.

Discretion

A discreet person exercises sound judgment when it comes to guarding private matters, using discretion in both his words and actions. What makes discretion so important is a little reality of life called *human nature*. To the extent we ignore this reality, we invite bad results into our lives.

It's human nature for people to want that which is least accessible to them and to be indifferent about that which is most available to them. To the degree you overexpose yourself, you become an inflated commodity, which in turn causes a devaluation of you in the eyes of others. Neither you nor I have anything to say about it; it's human nature that controls the issue.

In his book, *Power*, Michael Korda bluntly states, "No matter who you are, the basic truth is that your interests are nobody else's concern." The most poorly received words in the English language are *I, me,* and *my*. Some people display an almost childish naïveté in this regard, appearing to believe that everyone in the world is interested in the wart on their big toe or the fact that their dog had puppies last week. The well-adjusted individual separates himself from such self-centered fantasies early in life. In fact, one of life's great crises is coming to grips with the reality that our affairs simply aren't that important to others.

Inundating people with your problems is an especially self-destructive lack-of-discretion habit. Human nature makes it a certainty that it's a practice will badly tarnish your image with those unlucky souls who are on the listening end. Also, fewer people will want to deal with you, because it's human nature for others to keep their distance from those enshrouded by problems. The more you talk about your problems, the worse your chances of attracting positive people, which makes it that much harder to solve those problems. Even if someone is a good friend, it's a grave mistake to babble on endlessly about the details of your private life, because familiarity really does breed contempt.

Likewise, it's a lack of discretion to announce your plans to the world. There are too many envious and malevolent people out there who would just love to see you trip (preferably breaking three or four toes in the process). If your plans should yield the results you're hoping for, the world will hear about them soon enough. But, horror of horrors, if you should completely flop, why give card-carrying members of the World Order of Malevolent Mammals something else to cheer about?

Avoid revealing the heart of your enterprise to more people than are absolutely necessary to bring about its success. He who postpones declaring his purpose, particularly if it involves a major undertaking, envelopes his actions in a veil of mystery that commands respect. A plan fully declared is rarely well thought of and is fair game for criticism. Instead of arousing universal expectations, let people wonder and watch.

This is especially true when you're confident you have a deal wrapped up. It's the height of indiscretion to celebrate prematurely. Again, the surest way to invite trouble into your life and get malevolent people thinking about possible ways to derail you is to spout off about results prematurely. Never confuse the term *almost done* with the word *done*. There's a big difference between the two. **Real-World Rule No. 224: You're not through until you've crossed all the t's and dotted all the i's, and the check has cleared the bank.**

Unfortunately, there's no such thing as a smooth closing. Like a good pass receiver, you should acquire the habit of looking the pass into your hands before celebrating. I learned this lesson very early in my career when I managed to line up financing to build an apparel factory in Glenville, West Virginia. After working on the deal for months, the time finally came when I was able to get everyone involved to agree to a closing date. I was so excited, I was already counting the profits I was going to be earning in the coming years.

Having only recently completed my journey through the Age of Infinite Wisdom, I boasted to everyone who would listen (an order taker at McDonald's, two derelicts on a park bench, and an attorney from Zimbabwe) about my deal. At that early stage of my career, I wasn't familiar with the immortal words of that legendary Italian philosopher, Yogi Berractitus, who warned: "It ain't over till it's over."

You think you know the finale, right? Well, to guess this one correctly, you'd have to be a closet sadist. The day before the closing, I received a call from the secretary of the gentleman who was the key person in the financing of the project. Would you believe that she was calling to tell me her boss had suffered a fatal heart attack sitting at his desk—just twenty-four hours before the papers were to be signed and the money was to change hands? I was stunned. I'm telling you, some people will do anything to kill a deal!

Even when a deal does close (and, contrary to popular belief, it really does happen now and then), you still should avoid yakking to the world about how you managed to pull it off. Much cooler to let people scratch their heads in awe. As Don Shimoda said in Richard Bach's *Illusions*, "Learn what the magician knows and it's not magic anymore."

Genuineness

Genuineness is a matter of cultivating the habit of consciously trying to advertise your true self. The reality is that each of us is on stage, to one degree or another, throughout our lives. Just as it's impossible to be honest 100 percent of the time, neither is it possible for anyone to be himself always and completely. However, that doesn't mean a person should not *strive* to be himself, because, even then, he will still fall short of the mark.

There's at least one serious problem with being "on" too much of the time—or to too of an extreme: Not only do you continually run into yourself (in disguise) coming around every corner, but those who might like the real you won't get the opportunity to discover who you really are. The reason this is such a serious problem is that the biggest human relations dividends are reaped when you meet others who are most like you, both in your business and personal life.

Following is another nonbusiness example that I believe illustrates what I mean, and one in which the moral is equally applicable to financial situations.

In 1976, I was invited to a New Year's Eve party, and was wavering on whether or not to attend. I really dislike New Year's Eve parties, because I don't drink, don't dance, don't like to stay up late, and refuse to kiss strangers. I know, I know, you're thinking I'm not very exciting—and you're right.

Finally, Fate grabbed me by the throat and pulled me out the door and into my car, started the motor, and took me to the party. I stumbled around in my usual suave and sophisticated manner, exchanging pleasantries with total strangers and slowly losing the battle to keep my smile pasted on. People must have thought I had landed from the Planet Square, because I seemed to be the only male in attendance who didn't have my shirt unbuttoned to the waist, wasn't dangling seven pounds of fake gold from my neck, and didn't have coiffed locks reaching down to my shoulders. Throughout the hip Seventies, I stubbornly retained my Tommy Smothers hair style, to the great amusement of all who met me.

I should also explain that during the previous twelve months I had made a commitment to myself to grow up and start dressing and acting like a middle-aged adult—which you must admit is a huge challenge for a fully grown man in Los Angeles. I was determined to be the real Robert Ringer, no matter how out of place I might feel in any given situation.

About an hour after midnight, I was fumbling my way toward the front door, looking forward to the solitude of my humble abode, when I happened to catch a glimpse of a face—the most beautiful face I had ever seen—across the room. My heart started jumping around in my chest like a pachinko ball, and I seriously considered taking a drink. She was sitting and talking to another young lady, and not only was she beautiful, she also was smiling nonstop.

"What should I do? How do I make contact with her?" I frantically asked myself.

"Don't panic," the little character inside my wildly gyrating brain cautioned, "just be yourself."

Be myself? That was too much to think about. This was a situation that required immediate action. As I continued to stare at her through the crowd, wild thoughts bombarded my mind. Perhaps I should extend my arm toward her and break into "Some enchanted evening, you will see a stranger?"

"But what if I trip just as I get to her? What if she looks at me like I'm crazy, and gets up and leaves? Maybe I should jump up on the pillar behind her and break into something more upbeat, like 'Singin' In the Rain.' No, I might fall off, then I'd really look stupid."

Acutely aware that time was running out on an opportunity to meet my lifetime fantasy, I pulled myself together, patted my Smotherscut for unruly hairs, and marched resolutely toward her through the raucous, dancing crowd.

"I'll just be myself," I thought, "then take her insulting response in stride."

Within seconds, the moment arrived. Sitting next to her, I blurted out one of the great romantic lines of all time: "Hi!"

As I mentally braced myself in anticipation of her sharp-tongued response, this lovely female looked at me, displayed an incredible affidavit smile, and, in the most cheerful voice imaginable, answered, "Hi!"

I was so taken aback that I didn't know how to react at first. After all, this was the land of gold chains and leased Mercedes. Girls at parties weren't supposed to smile and be friendly—at least not until they checked your financial statement and film credits. Then, if all the paperwork was in order and the female was impressed, she might be willing to exchange ten minutes' worth of sarcastic conversation with you.

"What's going on here?" I asked my little friend roaming about inside my skull. "Who in the world is this happy mermaid, anyway?"

"Just be yourself, stupid, and don't blow it," he admonished me.

She was the first female I had met in Freakland in years who displayed an obvious abundance of self-confidence and self-esteem. No defensiveness; no sarcasm; no demands that the other person submit a typewritten résumé. In this little corner of our planet, such an attitude is considered way out of the mainstream, even somewhat bizarre.

"What's your name?" "Where are you from?" Normal, simple questions, with no thought given to how they might sound. Just honest, corny, straightforward stuff. It was great.

All I can remember is four hours of sitting and talking . . . walking around and talking . . . laughing and talking . . . and talking some more. When I finally departed at 5 a.m., there was no doubt in my mind that I had just met my future wife. Thirty-seven years have passed since that extraordinary New Year's Eve chance meeting, and my wife is still smiling, still the most natural, pure, kind, and considerate human being I have ever known. She comes the closest I've seen to a person who is never on stage. She's just as happy and real in private as she is in public. She's sincere and caring whether she's dealing with a high society matriarch or a clerk in a dilapidated shop in a Mexican pueblo.

As you can imagine, my wife and I have talked many times about our initial meeting, and we agree that had I tried to mimic the army of male mutants in attendance, fondling a gold chain and smirking as I approached her, it would have been a very short conversation. She would have had no idea what I was really like. Talk about a big payoff, this was one that dramatically changed my life for the better, and it was a direct result of practicing the habit of being genuine.

The moral? Always remember that the hardest way to impress people is to *try* to impress people. You have to merit respect and let it come naturally. As a rule, the least amount of respect and praise will come your way when actively seek them. Where you get into trouble is when you start trying to be someone other than who you really are. People may or may not like who you really are, but they will *never* like you for trying to be someone other than who you are.

Graciousness

Few things pay greater dividends in the area of human relations than the habit of exercising graciousness. What's so hard to understand is that even though it's simple to be kind and cordial to others, we live in a very ungracious world.

This thought first struck me about thirty years ago when I sent personalized, initialed Lucite paperweights to about fifty business acquaintances as Christmas gifts. I hadn't given any conscious thought to the recipients responding to my relatively expensive gifts when I sent them out, but when one person did call to thank me, human nature set in. Because one person—and one person only—did take the trouble to thank me, it got me to thinking about the other forty-none who didn't. With a response like this, I began to wonder what the feedback might have been had I sent the same people live tarantulas. So, when the next Christmas rolled around . . . just kidding.

Now, you might be thinking, "Well, your main reason for sending the gifts shouldn't have been to receive thanks from the people you sent them to." Aside and apart from the fact that, as I stated, I hadn't given any conscious thought to the recipients of my gifts responding in any way, what my motives may or may not have been completely misses the point. Regardless of my intent, the one individual who did take the trouble to thank me stood head and shoulders above the field.

Had that individual been selling insurance, or office furniture, or any other product or service for which I was in the market, can you imagine what an easy sale I would have been for him? That's the real lesson to be learned from this little story. The person who makes a habit of a simple action like displaying gratitude can't help but to reap benefits down the road, even if that isn't his main objective. Kind of like the invisible hand of the market place.

Refinement

Being refined is a matter of having good taste. There's nothing that breeds bad human relations as easily and quickly as being uncouth, rude, or vulgar.

To paraphrase an excellent example given by Zig Ziglar, in America a man is free to sport a Mohawk hairdo, dye it pink, wear a feathered earring in one ear, and spew out profanities. By the same token, employers are free not to hire him. By stretching his freedom to prove he can be as vulgar-looking as he desires, such a person also disqualifies himself from 90 percent or more of the employment opportunities that might otherwise be available to him. It's not a very pragmatic approach to life.

A few years ago, a young lady who had worked for me for only a few months asked if she could speak with me to air some grievances. I agreed to hear her out, whereupon she sat down and began to talk. After a few minutes of complaining that "Sue is doing this" and "Sally isn't doing that" (all about as relevant to her job as her ability to mud wrestle), she said, "I don't mind doing extra work, but I don't like being (expletive) over by everyone in the office." Suddenly, my anesthetized mind came out of its trance, I blinked, my jaw dropped open in awe, and I asked in wonderment, "What did you just say?"

To my amazement, I had heard right the first time. This young, lovely, all-American female—the archetypal girl next door—had just laid on her employer, whom she barely knew, a vulgar remark that I previously had heard come only from truck drivers, construction workers, and attorneys. My response was in the tradition of the late Vince Lombardi. I immediately traded this unrefined woman-child to the Atlanta Falcons for a a used IBM Selectric typewriter, a file cabinet, and a box of felt-tipped pens. Other than that, all it took was a smile, a severance check, and a good-luck wish. This young woman is free to say the same thing to any other employer if she so desires—and, in turn, that employer is also free to write her a severance check (although, in our current decadent legal environment, that admittedly is becoming more difficult to do).

All this, however, is a huge plus for you. The fact that we live in a society infested with rudeness and bad taste practically guarantees that a little thing like displaying good manners will win you the hearts and pocketbooks of prospects and clients. Simple, mannerly habits like saying "thank you" and "please" are mentally noted by others, especially by those who themselves practice good manners. And the people most likely to add value to your life are those who are refined and who appreciate refinement in others. When it comes to good human relations, refinement is another excellent insurance policy against failure. It's a habit that may not be important to everyone, but it will never offend anyone.

Responsibility

There's nothing more irritating than having to deal with a chronological adult whose responsibility level is equivalent to that of a twelve-year-old child. There are many ways in which a person can act irresponsible, but for our purposes I'm referring to irresponsibility as it relates to commitments. In the broadest of terms, the key to being a responsible person is to be found in the answer to a simple question: Do you do what you say you're going to do? This can be as seemingly insignificant as calling people back when you say you're going to, or going through with a business deal once you've verbally agreed to do so. (Note: Not returning phone calls is ungracious; not calling someone when you've committed to doing so is irresponsible.)

As you can see, there's a bit of moral overlap here, because, in the purest sense of the word, it's also dishonest not to do what you've told someone you're going to do. But even if you don't agree with the moral aspect, there's no question that the practice of keeping your commitments plays to your benefit. As with people not returning phone calls, I refuse to deal with someone once he's failed to keep a commitment, whether it's getting a package of materials to me by a certain date or failing to show up for a meeting. The only exception to this policy is if (1) the person calls me—preferably in advance—and explains why he was (or is) not able to perform as promised, and (2) it's my first such negative experience with him.

The key to keeping your commitments, of course, is to be careful about making commitments in the first place. Better to have someone be unhappy about your refusal to commit than to be mad over your failure to execute. Word travels fast when it comes to responsibility, so pay close attention to your performance in this area. It's a simple habit to practice, and one you can count on to pay big dividends if adhered to on a consistent basis.

Self-Sufficiency

Self-sufficiency is a trait that evokes admiration from others, which results in people wanting to do business with you. The person with an expansive mental paradigm is likely to be self-sufficient, because his resourcefulness gives him the capacity to find alternative solutions rather than appeal to others for help.

Unfortunately, the first thing most people think of when confronted with an obstacle is to ask for assistance, and as soon as that happens, their posture is diminished. When you ask someone for a favor, you should understand that you're incurring a debt. It may not be verbally stated, but it's there—

in the accounts receivable section of the other person's Favors Book—just as surely as if you had signed a promissory note. This in turn brings about two negatives:

First, because you have a limited credit line with every person with whom you come in contact, you have to be careful not to use up valuable credit on situations that aren't truly important. The prudent individual always saves some credit for a rainy day. Second, if the accounts-payable section of *your* Favors Book becomes too great, you're likely to find yourself making more and more decisions that others want you to make, and that results in a lack of freedom.

Even if you work for someone else, the more you make it a habit to act on your own initiative, taking action without waiting for others to guide you, the more likely you are to get ahead. I like the way Peter Ueberroth, former commissioner of baseball, put it when he said, "Authority is 20 percent given and 80 percent taken."

Tactfulness

The first step toward being tactful is to nurture the habit of erasing negative and abrasive words and phrases from your vocabulary. You create obstacles to getting the results you want when you use words and phrases like, "There's one *problem* that has to be resolved first;" "There's *no negotiation* on that point;" "You're *wrong*;" "*I don't care* whether you like it or not;" or, "That's a *lie*."

Good human relations require that you employ much more tact than this when it comes to language, such as, "There's only one *issue* that needs to be resolved, and *I don't see any problem with being able accomplish that*;" "*You could be right*, but I'd like to review the facts one more time;" "*I certainly want you to feel good about this deal*, but let me explain why I think this is the best way to handle it;" or, "*That may be true*, but I'd still like to present the facts as I see them."

The first sampling of phrases could be the basis for a book titled *How to Lose Friends and Infuriate People.* The second sampling is the basis for superior human relations and is infinitely more likely to lead to positive results.

The more you directly challenge the words or actions of another party, the less likely you are to get what you're after. I remember attending a meeting in New York, the purported purpose of which was to resolve some differences that I and another party had been having with several principals in a partnership with which we were dealing. One of the partners had signed an agreement with us that the other partners maintained was not legally binding. After thoroughly researching the law, we were convinced that they had no legal grounds to stand on, but pragmatism motivated us to try to work amiably with them to arrive at an acceptable compromise.

Shortly after we arrived at the office of one of the partners, we sat down at his conference table, and, to our surprise, the first words out of his mouth, in an extremely hostile tone, were, "All right, let's not beat around the bush. Before we even agree to discuss the terms of a possible new deal, you either sign a rescission of the original agreement or we march down to the court house and start litigation."

Yikes! It was Ho Chi Minh in a dress shirt and silk suit. The ensuing fifteen minutes almost turned into a brawl. I was lucky I didn't get a broken nose. After privately pondering a number of solutions to the surprise dilemma we faced—such as firebombing Ho Chi Minh's office or pouring a bottle of Liquid Paper on his wig—I decided to fight ignorance with intelligent tact and began the long journey toward a civilized meeting by saturating the air with congenial words. Ultimately, we succeeded in overcoming the gauche behavior of our Hitlerian host and managed to work out an amiable solution to the problem.

Why in the world would anyone who was in a negotiating position of weakness begin a meeting by throwing verbal punches? It could have been the age-old strategy of attacking when you know you're in the wrong or when your posture is weak, hoping that it will throw the other side off balance; or it could have been a case of ego overriding pragmatism; or it could have been nothing more than abject ignorance. Regardless of the reason, it's amateurish and imprudent to come out swinging. When it comes to negotiating, diplomacy and a pair of deuces beat hostility and four aces every time.

A tactful individual makes it a habit to avoid challenging people, even if he feels sure they're wrong. If it isn't something really crucial, pragmatism dictates that you let it slide. The cost of proving you're right can often be too high, especially if the provee is a customer or superior. The instant gratification of flaunting the fact that you were right can prove to be fatal in the long term. At a minimum, the cost of proving you're right usually results in a loss of allies. It's the proverbial case of winning the battle but losing the war.

Tolerance
Tolerance is one of the most difficult human relations habits to master, because it requires looking past our own beliefs and perceptions and respecting another's right to embrace different beliefs and perceptions. It doesn't mean we have to agree with the other person, just that we grant him the right to think for himself. Though we're all guilty of intolerance to one degree or another, carried to an extreme, it's a surefire way to undercut human relations. Intolerant individuals often display open contempt for people and things that don't fit within the guidelines of their thinking patterns. Bigotry is the end station of the Intolerance Express.

One of the keys to nurturing the habit of tolerance is to simultaneously cultivate the habit of flexibility. Being flexible can make your journey through life much easier, and far more enjoyable, than if your view of the world is rigid. Only zealots and those living through the Age of Infinite Wisdom are totally inflexible. When you're a child, it seems as though everything is black and white. Then, at about twenty-five, things start to become a little gray; at thirty, they become grayer still; then, finally, at about forty, you feel as though you're looking at the whole world through Los Angeles smog.

The reality is that we live in an anti-Ayn Rand world. I was one of the last holdouts when it came to Ayn Rand's inflexible view of the world, a view she expressed so eloquently in such bestselling novels as *Atlas Shrugged* and *The Fountainhead*. I was like one of those World War II Japanese soldiers they used to find hiding in the mountains in the Philippines every ten years or so, the guy who peeked his head out of the bushes and asked, in a shaky voice, "Is it over yet?"

After years of being certain that every word Ayn Rand wrote was unequivocally right, I woke up one morning and realized that I was covered with bumps and bruises. Why? Because I had been living through something called *real life*. Repeatedly, I would go back and reread *Atlas Shrugged* and *The Fountainhead* to try to figure out what was wrong, until one day I finally said to myself, "Hey, this is great stuff! And if I ever move to another planet that's full of Henry Reardens and Howard Roarks and Dagny Taggarts (fictional characters from Ayn Rand's novels), it's going to be fantastic. But the problem is, I'm not living on another planet right now. This is planet Earth, and there are no Dagny Taggarts or Howard Roarks here. The closest we ever came was Gary Cooper."

A one-time close confidant of Ayn Rand's once told me, "Do you know what Ayn Rand's problem was? She thought you were mentally deranged if you dared to disagree with 1 percent of her philosophy." Ayn Rand's inflexible, intolerant attitude was evident to anyone who closely followed her career. As much as I admired Ayn Rand as an intellectual, it saddened me to see her die an obviously unhappy, lonely woman. She seemingly felt it was necessary to mold the world in her own image in order to be content. How would you like *your* happiness to depend upon *your* ability to mold the world in *your* image? Talk about a tough occupation, try going into that business sometime. That's what's known as masochistic intolerance.

To help develop the habit of tolerance, when a person makes a mistake, or offends you, or acts in ways that are not to your liking, remind yourself that you don't know what happened to him before he left home that morning, let alone the inside story of his entire life. Behind the face of every human being, deep within the recesses of his gray matter, is a Hollywood tale to be told. Each and every one of us carries our own secret, heavy burdens through life, and those burdens directly impact on our actions. It's the height of good human relations to take this reality into consideration when dealing with others.

Value for Value

The concept of value for value is the foundation for all sound, harmonious human relationships. Value for value is another way of saying "win-win." It's a real tragedy that surveys consistently reveal that most people believe success comes only at the expense of others. In today's age of envy, it's hard for the average person to grasp the principle that the surest way to succeed is to make certain that all parties to a transaction come out ahead.

As with all sound moral principles, making a habit of thinking value for value is also pragmatic. You rest so much better at night if you don't have to depend upon the gratitude of others for your just rewards. In fact, practicing the concept of value for value is the surest way to protect yourself in a business relationship. You can spend a fortune on legal fees and draw up a contract two feet thick, but the reality is that if you manipulate a situation in such a way that it ends up being an onerous deal for the other party, you'll only succeed in buying yourself a lawsuit. **Real-World Rule No. 322: Regardless of what a contract says, no one will get up every morning and go to work for nothing, especially if the other parties to a venture are profiting from it.**

Value for value is the antithesis of force. Force always loses in the real world, as evidenced by the fates of political dictators around the globe, from Adolph Hitler to Idi Amin to Bashar al-Assad. Both nature and the human will tenaciously resist force. The hopelessness of using force as a means of achieving cooperation can be witnessed in all areas of business.

For example, to the extent an employer utilizes force against employees, not only will they resist him and find creative ways to defy his iron-fisted approach, but, like the proverbial rats abandoning a sinking ship, they will turn on him or desert him when his business hits the skids. Abraham Lincoln stated it both accurately and succinctly when he said: "Force is all-conquering, but its victories are short lived." Force is not in harmony with nature; actions based on value for value are.

Once you develop the habit of thinking in terms of value for value, you'll find it's quite easy to make money. All you need to do is abide by the following value-for-value rules:

1. If you want more, make yourself worth more.

2. Concentrate on quality and service first, and profit will follow as a natural result.

3. Always give more than you expect to get in return.

With respect to number two, when I was in my late teens, I operated a fruit stand in the summer months. My dad, the most go-the-extra-mile, customer-oriented human being I've ever known, once noticed that I was busy trying to make my fruit displays perfect while a customer patiently stood by and waited for me to finish. After the customer left, my Dad severely chastised me for my indifference toward the customer, and told me two things that I never forgot:

First, when a customer comes in, stop whatever you're doing and give him all your attention. Second, never argue with a customer, no matter how irrational his statements may be. In the world of business, my dad said that the definition of a customer is someone who wants to buy what you're selling, and who therefore is incapable of being wrong.

Which brings us to today's world of laziness, incompetence, negligence, and ignorance. How lucky you are that you have the right attitude, or at least (hopefully) have made a commitment to develop the right attitude. Since so few people have a customer-oriented attitude, the competition is slim. Imagine how difficult it would have been to succeed during an age when a majority of people were customer-service oriented?

The attitude of an employee toward his employer, as well as the attitude of all representatives of a business toward their customers, should be: "How may I be of the greatest service to you?" This kind of refreshing attitude may sound anachronistic, but it virtually guarantees success. In other words, the fact that most people don't operate in this manner is to your great advantage if you do. Every time you run into rudeness, inconvenience, poor service, or indifference toward customers, you're witnessing a business that is actively inviting competition. On the other hand, if *you* maintain the habit of being customer-oriented, you can virtually eliminate competition.

The Adventures of Ms. Snippy

Some years ago, I recall stopping in to pick up my laser printer at a computer store where I had taken it to be repaired. The jivey young lass (Ms. Snippy) behind the counter appeared to be eighteenish. I gave her my repair receipt, whereupon she called a serviceman to bring my printer to the front counter. So far, no problem. But, hold it, my paper tray was missing.

When I called this to Ms. Snippy's attention, she snapped back, "You didn't bring in a paper tray with your printer. I know, because I handled the order."

"No," I said with a smile, "I know I brought it in, because I thought about it ahead of time and decided I had better bring it just in case the service department needed it."

"And I know you didn't," she retorted with a juvenile sneer, "because I would have remembered."

Now I had a serious problem on my hands, because everyone knows that the memories of eighteen-year-olds are infallible. The serviceman invited me to come in the back room with him so we could see if the missing tray was inadvertently left lying around. Ms. Snippy followed close behind, intent on protecting her vested interest in the outcome. Unfortunately, there was no extra tray to be found. There were plenty of paper trays, but they all were inserted in other printers. Throughout the search, Ms. Snippy, in a nose-thumbing tone, kept repeating, "I told you that you didn't bring in a paper tray."

As I gently straight-armed Ms. Snippy to one side, I said to the serviceman, "Look, I don't want to be difficult, but the bottom line is that I did bring in my paper tray, and, though I hate to put it this way, I expect to go home with a paper tray, regardless of what you have to do to get me one." Over the near-violent objections of Ms. Snippy, the serviceman obliged me by taking a tray from another printer, whereupon I made my exit, the back of my neck burning from the flames shooting out of Ms. Snippy's nostrils.

Concerned that perhaps I had gone mad (What if I really didn't say "to go" five or ten times at the deli, and what if I really didn't bring in my paper tray?), when I got home I thoroughly searched my house for the missing paper tray. No luck. However, because the serviceman had been gracious to me, I took the trouble to call him the next day to let him know that I definitely did not have the other paper tray at my house. Before I could finish, he interrupted me and said, "Oh, just after you left, I found your tray. It was on a top shelf. Sorry for the inconvenience."

I don't know, maybe it's just something about minimum-wage, eighteen-year-olds that I'm not equipped to handle . . .

Now, some people might be inclined to say that it's not the owner of the computer store who's at fault, that perhaps he thinks in terms of value-for-value service, even if his employees don't. Wrong! The owner who cares enough about his customers not only will take the trouble to instill his business philosophy in his employees, he'll also make certain they follow through on his policies. When it comes to bad service, it's *always* the owners fault.

The Great Catalyst

In this chapter, I touched on a number of positive human relations traits, but, in reality, there is no limit to the number of ways in which you can improve your ability to earn and retain the goodwill of others. There is no way to escape the reality that you have to deal with other people in order to succeed to any meaningful degree. Nor is there any escaping the reality that the more successful you are in getting others to cooperate with you, the easier it becomes to reach your goals. No matter how good you are at your business or profession, you'll always fall short of your aim if you fail to develop good human relations habits.

No one ever becomes perfect at the art of good human relations, but the good news is that it's within your power to improve at it every day of your life. And the better you become, the more you will attract others who appreciate people who practice good human relations. Remember, when you excel at the Human Relations Habit, you attract attractive human beings, and attractive human beings add value to your life. There is no better catalyst for getting results than gaining the goodwill of others.

If you already knew everything about human relations discussed in this chapter, all you have to do now is put your knowledge into practice on a consistent basis. When you do so, you'll be pleased to find that it becomes much easier to achieve what you want out of life.

CHAPTER 7

THE SIMPLICITY HABIT

If it's true that we teach best those things we need to learn, I should be at my finest in this chapter. For as long as I can remember, I've carried on a ferocious battle against my obsessive-compulsive instincts in an effort to simplify my life. I used to think it was a deficit unique to me, but I've come to realize that everyone, to one degree or another, wrestles with the problem of trying to make his life less complicated.

It's really amazing how cavalierly we dissipate our most precious resource—time—by complicating our lives. Given a choice between doing something in a simple or complex manner, most people will tend to choose the complex way. Why? Who knows? Maybe human beings just love pain.

Whatever the reasons, experience has convinced me that, all other things being equal, simplicity is almost always the best approach when it comes to getting results. Over the past decade, I've begun to experience the delicious effects of simplicity, and I must say that I'm perplexed by how I found so many ways to complicate my life in bygone years. What a cathartic feeling to rid oneself of thoughts, projects, and activities that clutter his mind and his life while contributing little or nothing to the achievement of his goals.

It's impossible to place a value on a clear mind, because when you cleanse it of the thousands of trivial thoughts that continually bombard it, it makes it possible for you to concentrate on the kind of thoughts that have the potential to make a real difference in your life. Most of us are drowning in a sea of unimportant to marginally important papers. I long ago concluded that the reason I kept tens of thousands of letters, notes, contracts, memos, and other papers neatly filed away and meticulously indexed is because I feared I might someday have to prove a point to someone. The problem, however, was that I eventually reached a point of diminishing returns; i.e., I ended up with so much paper that I had difficulty finding the documents that really were important.

Years of experience have convinced me that only a tiny fraction of the papers I saved ever were needed, and even then I found that the consequences of not having a document when it was needed (the document you need is almost always the one you can't find) were never as grim as I had imagined. It was a losing proposition from every aspect. It makes one take seriously Buddha's observation that "all unhappiness is caused by attachment."

Overcommitment

In the previous chapter, I alluded to how I used to have a problem giving someone a firm and immediate *no* if I didn't want to go along with something requested of me. I also stated that the key to keeping your commitments is to be careful about making commitments. The only thing worse than not saying *no* immediately is to say *yes* immediately. If you're too generous or too fast on the trigger with your *yes's*, it's likely to result in endless frustration and an unnecessarily complicated life. In my second book, *Looking Out For #1*, I offered a simple antidote to this universal problem, and it's still the best one I know of: Learn to say no politely and pleasantly, but immediately and firmly. This is a remarkably easy-to-master habit that can dramatically simplify your life.

It's hard enough to avoid spreading yourself too thin just keeping up with the things you absolutely have to do and want to do—such as working, sleeping, exercising, reading, spending time with your family, and enjoying various kinds of recreation— without committing to an excess of marginal projects in a hopeless effort to accommodate everyone. **Real-World Rule No. 231: Don't be so much to everyone else that you become nothing to yourself.**

The Penny-ante Trap

The Penny-ante Trap is the inability to overlook minor, perceived injustices, especially when they involve money. Remember that even though life doesn't always seem fair, you do have the power to control how you react to its unfairnesses. Don't spend hours—and certainly not days or weeks—trying to rectify a wrong that involves a relatively small amount of money. To keep from complicating your life, it's important to develop the habit of immediately asking yourself if the amount of time you'll have to invest to remedy what you perceive to be an injustice is really worth it. It's a real sucker trap, and the smaller the mind, the more likely the person is to get caught in it.

I recently had a friend ask my advice regarding a situation that was giving her a lot of angst. A rather nasty beauty salon operator had purchased some beauty products from her, only because the wholesaler he normally ordered from had gone out of business. My friend was reluctant to sell to him because she had had problems with him in a couple of earlier encounters.

Sure enough, about two months after he purchased the products, he called her and, in a hostile tone, demanded that she take back the items he had not sold and immediately issue him a refund. Her company's policy, which was stated on its invoices, was not to accept any returns unless they were made within thirty days of purchase, and then only if the products still were in their original cartons. If these two conditions were met, the customer could then receive a credit toward other purchases. The invoices clearly stated that cash refunds would not be issued under any circumstances.

Not only was the hostile salon operator way past the thirty-day limit for returning merchandise, he also did not have the original cartons. On top of that, he was demanding a cash refund. My friend wanted to know what I would do if I were her. I asked her whether she liked the salon operator enough to give him part of her life. "Of course not," she responded.

"Well, if he's as hostile as you claim," I continued, "he'll drain you of an enormous amount of time and energy before the matter is resolved, and, regardless of the outcome, you will have lost that time and energy forever. Since you couldn't care less about him, the only relevant question is, 'How much do you value your own time and energy?'"

It's back to the cost of proving you're right. The purpose of life isn't to see how often you can prove you're right. The purpose of life is to live. When you run into an ugly situation like the one just described, get in the habit of weighing the realities carefully before taking a tough stand. Who needs the aggravation? You should be spending most of your time working on opportunities and creative projects, not penny-ante issues.

The Dally Dummy

For years, it drove me nuts trying to figure out why so many people worked fewer hours than I did, yet did much better financially. One day, I happened to read an article that said numerous studies indicated that the most successful people are not workaholics. What they're good at is achieving the best possible results in the shortest period of time. That one hurt real bad. When I looked in the mirror this time, I saw a real-life Dally Dummy staring back at me. Simply too much dallying—too many paper clips and staples, too many letters being redrafted, too many copies of documents being made, too many labels being neatly affixed, too many details that, in the overall scheme of things, didn't really matter.

Since I've become semi-normal, I've been fascinated by the reality that very few things in daily life really matter that much; i.e., most things simply don't have the potential to make a significant impact on the quality of a person's life. Now my first objective every morning is to eliminate as many projects as possible. Hands down, the fastest way to complete any task is to simply cross it off your To Do list. However, even if it isn't feasible to eliminate a project, you should still make it a habit to simplify it and get it off your desk as quickly as possible. A little discipline like allowing yourself to handle a piece of paper only once can have a major impact on the quality of your results—and your life.

To simplify my own life, I've attacked the Dally Dummy within me in many ways, one of the most important of which is to make it a regular habit to follow the "Three Gets." When I enter my office each morning, I consciously think to myself: "Get in. Get it done. Get out!" It may sound simplistic, but accidentally stapling my tie to a letter as a result of dallying is even worse.

Why do the Three Gets work? Because of the truth inherent in Parkinson's First Law: Work expands to fill the time available for its completion. Once you've mentally absorbed this reality, and cultivated the habit of guarding against it, you've practically bought yourself a whole new life.

The Meeting Trap

Simplicity ends where meetings begin. A Dally Dummy takes to meetings like a play-by-play sports announcer clings to clichés.

When someone requests a meeting with you, the first question in your mind should be, "Is this meeting really necessary?" And when someone does convince you that a meeting is necessary, demand that he get to the point. Refuse to allow any meeting to drag on beyond its useful life.

Remember the tradeoff: If you're in a meeting, you can't be working on creative projects that have the potential to produce financial results. Contrary to the erroneous belief harbored by a majority of people, all the great ideas and discoveries throughout history began as a creative seed planted in the mind of a single individual. John Steinbeck alluded to this in his novel *East of Eden*, when he said, ". . .The group can build and extend [an idea], but the group never invents anything. The preciousness lies in the lonely mind of a man."

The Plight of the Supernothing

One of the most crucial of all simplicity habits is to concentrate on what you do best, and let others do the rest. Remember, the objective is to get results, not see how many aptitudes you can flaunt. Too many aptitudes lead to the emergence of that great Supernothing within each of us, and thus to an unnecessarily complicated life. I'm convinced it is one of the chief causes of failure.

People often forget that we live in a division-of-labor society, where it not only isn't necessary to do everything yourself, it isn't even necessary to understand how something works to use it. You don't need an intricate knowledge of automobile engines to drive a car. You don't need to understand the transmission of television signals to use a television set. It usually will cost you a lot more in wasted time *not* to pay for someone else's services than it will to do something yourself that you aren't qualified to do.

This lesson hit me between my right and left forebrains some thirty years ago when I bought my first personal computer. Have you ever tried to read a computer manual? Day after day, I relentlessly studied the manual that came with my computer, trying to suppress my frustration and stubbornly believing that if I just stuck with it, sooner or later I would learn how to turn on the computer.

Finally, just as I was on the verge of being committed to the Computer Institute for Low-tech Mental Arthritics, the solution struck me. I looked in the Yellow Pages (How's that for dated?) and called a computer instructor who specialized in word processing. I told him my interest in computers was limited to writing books and organizing speeches, so I was interested in learning how to use a word-processing program. I also emphasized that I did *not* want to learn anything about computers, per se.

Would you believe that the instructor had me functional in about an hour, and reasonably proficient by the end of the day? And after the second (and last) lesson, I was breezing. Now I'm so fast I should be outlawed. But guess what? I still don't know a whole lot about computers! Let others be computer experts if that's their objective. My objective is to write books and organize speeches, so for me a computer is only a means to an end.

The point is that any time spent working on projects that don't take advantage of your best talents is time inefficiently spent. The common term is *delegation*—parceling out jobs to others, whether those others be employees or outside people who you pay to do the work. Delegation is absolutely essential to a simple life, and at the heart of good delegation is the willingness to let go. For someone like me, that's somewhat of a challenge.

Most people make the mistake of trying to battle their deficiencies; instead they should hire out their deficiencies and nurture their skills. President Dwight Eisenhower once said that the mark of a good executive is when you're handed letters that you know you could have written better yourself, and you sign them anyway.

Merely telling someone to do something, however, does not constitute effective delegation. Implementing the following steps will go a long way toward helping you to excel at this art:

1. Tell people exactly what you want them to accomplish.

2. Let them be creative and find a way to accomplish it. In other words, don't try to solve your subordinates' problems for them. This means that you have to let go and allow other people to do it their way, at least within a reasonable framework.

3. Spot-check their work on a regular basis.

4. If their work is unsatisfactory, redirect them.

Getting in the habit of delegating pays exponential dividends by simplifying your life and increasing your balance sheet.

The Crux of the Issue

The late Joe Karbo, author of the much-publicized book, *The Lazy Man's Way to Riches*, was fond of saying that most people are too busy earning a living to make any money. What Karbo meant was that the average person never seems to find the time to work on the really important things, the creative projects that produce big payoffs. It is creativity, not hard work, that's at the heart of success in any field of endeavor. And in order for a person to have the time to engage in creative thinking, he must learn to work efficiently.

To do this, it's crucial to develop the habit of focusing on the crux of the issue. By *crux of the issue*, I'm talking about the point or points upon which success or failure rests. You must resist the temptation to get sidetracked by peripheral issues that cannot yield a payoff, no matter what their outcome.

In this regard, people often confuse the means with the end. Did you ever grind away at a project for hours, then look up and ask yourself, "Why am I doing this?" More often than not, the reason is that you got caught up in trying to make the details perfect, and, in the process, lost sight of what was your original objective. Many people spend most of their time working on details, hopelessly trying to make everything perfect.

Unfortunately, in the real world, such perfection doesn't produce meaningful results. To paraphrase Peter Drucker, you should concentrate on doing the right thing rather than doing things right. In other words, more important than the question of whether or not you're spending too much time on a project is the question: Should I be working on this project *at all?* Focusing on the crux of the issue requires an understanding of what's important to work on and what isn't.

You're probably familiar with the 80/20 Rule, which states that the average person spends 80 percent of his time on tasks and projects that produce 20 percent of his results. For example, did you ever notice that carelessly typed envelopes and shoddily wrapped packages with messy labels seem to arrive just as quickly as those that look as though they had been produced by Michelangelo? Though it can be a tough reality for a perfectionist to accept, the truth is that the aesthetics of an envelope or package simply don't matter. They have nothing whatsoever to do with the substance of the letter or package.

A person has a choice: He can spend his time wrapping packages to perfection or he can utilize his time working on important, creative projects. The latter produces financial results, while the former produces only high blood pressure. Fighting the 80/20 Rule is an ongoing battle, and to aid me in this battle, years ago I made the following sign and hung it on my office wall:

Does it matter?
If so, how much does it matter?

The reason I included the second question on the sign is because you can argue that everything matters to one extent or another, and that's true. But the more important question is, "How *much* does it matter?" It's the habit of asking myself this second question that continually reminds me to focus on the crux of every issue.

Looking at the crux of the issue in the broadest possible terms, the real question is: What do I need to do right now that will produce measurable, maximum results for me? Believe me, you don't have much time for anything else. Understanding this reality has a great deal to do with how hard—and how much— you have to work to get where you want to be in life.

The Ultimate Simplicity Formula

In 1980, after the publication of my third book, *Restoring the American Dream,* I was contacted by an elderly gentleman who wanted to buy a large quantity of the book in hardcover and start a grass-roots campaign to "change the course of Western Civilization." Several times he invited me to come to his home in Las Vegas, and, after finally concluding that he was, indeed, serious about his intentions (he had already purchased about five thousand copies of the book), I agreed to make the trip.

What happened after my arrival in Las Vegas was like something out of a science fiction movie. The elderly gentleman ("Paul") picked me up at the airport, then drove directly to an empty lot on the outskirts of the city. He then pulled into a driveway that was closed off by iron gates. After pausing for a moment, the electric gates swung open and we proceeded to drive to a vacant area, the most notable feature of which was a cluster of giant-size boulders. Paul then stopped his car near the boulders, at which point I began to wonder what I was getting myself into.

After we got out of the car, Paul approached the boulders, waved his hand, and said aloud, "Open Sesame." Just like in the movie, one of the large boulders slowly began to swing open. He had me follow him into a dark hallway inside the pile of boulders, which I (nervously) did. After a few steps, we came to—of all things—an elevator. As I stepped into the elevator, the thought crossed my mind that I might never again be seen alive. I might end up being one of those people who mysteriously disappears, with not a trace of evidence left behind.

The elevator descended slowly, and after about twenty seconds came to a gentle stop. The door opened and I found myself in an underground paradise—beautiful landscaping, with trees, bushes, and flowers as authentic-looking as anything I had seen at Disneyland, a majestic home, a free-standing guest house, a rock-formed swimming pool and Jacuzzi, and many more wonders beyond anything a humble word hacker like myself could possibly describe.

After a tour of the vast underground grounds, we rested in the sprawling living room of Paul's home and chatted. He said he wanted to buy seventy thousand hardcover copies of *Restoring the American Dream*, and, out of the goodness of my heart, I agreed to sell them to him at a discount. As the conversation unfolded, I inferred that Paul's net worth was in the area of $500 million, and, at one point, I asked him, perhaps presumptuously, "Paul, how in the world did you ever accumulate such wealth?"

His answer was the essence of simplicity. He said, "You know, making money is really a very simple proposition. All you do is charge the highest price for your product or service that the market will bear, keep your expenses as low as possible, and in between is your profit."

Whereupon I suavely retorted, "Gaa . . . llee."

Indeed, Paul had never been involved in any kind of complex business or venture. Starting out as a one-man delivery service in the Brooklyn–New Jersey area fifty years earlier (with a used truck he had purchased for $100), he religiously followed his simple success formula, accumulated huge cash reserves, then continually multiplied his wealth by buying assets for cash, holding onto them until the market demand was sufficiently high, then selling them at substantial profits. (Yes, Paul is the same gentleman I described in Chapter 3, the one who lost his house during the Great Depression.)

The Other Side of the Coin

That meeting with Paul really opened my eyes. From that point on, I became conscious of how most people, including myself, unnecessarily complicate the process of making money. In particular, I never forgot the part of Paul's success formula that called for keeping your expenses as low as possible. Having won nine consecutive World High-Overhead titles at a relatively young age, I can tell you with certainty that high overhead is one of the easiest ways to complicate your existence.

In fact, in my previous life, I developed a reputation as a professional employer. By that, I mean I didn't produce a product or service; I just employed people. No matter what my circumstances were at any given time, I kept everyone on the payroll—marketing people, analysts, secretaries, receptionists, assistant receptionists, gophers . . . you name the job, and if I didn't have it, I'd create it for you. It was my own little welfare state. I managed to keep all my employees busy with make-work projects, which allowed them to continue drawing paychecks during even the worst of times.

It was absolutely great. My employees were able to afford the best tickets to ball games and concerts, eat at the finest restaurants, set aside money for vacations—nothing but the best for them.

What a contribution I made to society, because my employees didn't have to depend on Uncle Sam to take care of them. They had their own personal Uncle Dumb.

Unfortunately, every entrepreneur who has made this noble mistake has found out the hard way that there's one major flaw in the operating system: The dollars flow in only one direction; no one looks out for Uncle Dumb! Worse, through some remarkable quirk of human nature, gratitude quickly turns to hostility when you can no longer meet payroll—no matter how generous you were with your employees when the good times were rolling. (If all this causes some bad memories from your own past to resurface, you may want to take a break, retrieve your Employee Doll from the middle drawer of your desk and brush up on your dart throwing.)

There's a direct correlation between high overhead—and particularly high labor costs—and a complicated business life. Just as it's important to learn the habit of not dwelling on penny-ante matters, so, too, is it important to practice the habit of keeping overhead to a minimum.

A Lousy One Percent Profit

Everyone has heard the adage about not trying to reinvent the wheel, but I question how many people really take it to heart. We're living in an age of computers, satellites, and genetic technology, but five of the top-ten wealthiest Americans are descendants of Sam Walton, founder of Walmart Stores. And what did Sam Walton do to become so rich? The same thing that Jewish merchants were doing thousands of years ago in the Middle East and hundreds of years ago in Europe—"buying things for a dollar, selling them for two dollars, and making a lousy 1 percent profit."

Likewise, Holiday Inns merely adopted Howard Johnson's motel-chain idea and did a better job. White Castle was in business more than twenty years before Ray Kroc came along, but McDonald's borrowed its hamburger-chain concept and carried it to new heights. IBM was around for decades before Steve Jobs ever thought of Apple Computer. And all Century 21 did was find a new way to organize a business that had been in existence for centuries.

Real-World Rule No. 322: It's a lot simpler to follow a pioneer than be a pioneer. The easiest and most direct path to finding a marketable product or service is to modify a known success and improve on it.

Minding the Store

Nor do you have to think in terms of rapid expansion to strike it rich. The best example with which I am personally familiar is that of a long-time friend, Fred Hayman. Fred, a native of Switzerland, never finished high school, but managed to secure a job as a management apprentice at the Waldorf-Astoria Hotel in New York not too long after coming to the United States. In 1954, he transferred to Los Angeles, where he worked as a chef at the Beverly Hilton Hotel.

A short time later, Fred bought into a failing clothing store in Beverly Hills. His two partners ultimately wanted to close down the operation and cut their losses, but Fred instead bought them out. By his own admission, he knew nothing at all about the retail business, but he stayed with that one store, nurtured it like a mother hen, pampered his customers like no one ever before had done, and was on the premises every day, overseeing all aspects of his operation.

The store's reputation for quality and service became so well known that, without ever opening so much as a second branch, Giorgio virtually became a household name nationwide. Capitalizing on the remarkable name identification he had built, in 1982 Fred launched Giorgio Perfume. The fragrance was marketed through prestigious department stores across the country and became an immediate sensation. Five years later, he sold his perfume company to Avon for a tidy $165 million.

Fred Hayman shattered a lot of entrepreneurial myths with his one-store mega-success. The key lesson is that it's not so much whether you have one store or one thousand stores, it's your methodology that determines the bottom line. Even Ray Kroc said that initially he didn't give much to franchising McDonald's, that his main focus was on making his first unit operate as smoothly as possible. He explained that once you have a single operation running efficiently and profitably, nationwide expansion is a relatively simple process.

To their detriment, many entrepreneurs focus far too much on expansion at the outset, failing to take the necessary time and effort to lay a solid foundation upon which to build. **Real-World Rule No. 208: The more rapid the expansion, particularly in the early years, the less likely a business is to succeed.** A partial corollary to this is: The long-term success of a venture tends to be inversely proportional to the amount of immediate success, or perceived immediate success, of the venture.

Get in the habit of working hard to find simple deals, then find simple ways to profit from them.

The Complexity of Greener Grass

Another mistake with which I am all too familiar is believing that a fatiguing travel schedule is a key to making money. In truth, it's not necessary to perpetually crisscross the country to find good deals, because there are probably more than you can handle in your own backyard.

I recall the sad tale of an acquaintance from yesteryear who owned a large home on a prestigious street along the ocean in the Los Angeles area. Herb had been a typical wheeler-dealer builder for many years, continually traveling the country and building monuments to himself in the forms of bigger and bigger high-rise office buildings and apartment complexes. I say "typical," because in the end, like most high-flying builders, he went belly up.

Years later, we had occasion to discuss his trials and tribulations, and he said to me, "You know, I spent a fortune while enduring all the discomfort and inconvenience associated with traveling to distant cities to develop large projects. It was a never-ending nightmare of hassling with skycaps, ticket agents, stewardesses, taxi drivers, and bellmen, checking in and out of hotels, and all the other horrors that go with business travel, and it turned out to be all for nothing.

"What's so ironic about it is that if I had just stayed home all those years and taken a one-hour walk up and down my own street every day, keeping an eye open for properties that were for sale, I could have made millions with very little effort. All I would have needed to do was buy up virtually every property that came on the market. During the years I was wheeling and dealing all over the country, the real estate on my street increased in value ten times or more."

In relating this story to you, I'm not suggesting that there isn't money to made in distant cities. What I am saying is that, all other things being equal, you should try the simplest path first. Carefully check out the deals in your own backyard before venturing cross country in search of that ever-elusive greener grass.

Make It Easy on Yourself

In Chapter 1, I alluded to a marketing maxim that says: If you want to do well, sell people what they need; if you want to get rich, sell people what they want. However, I should caution you that if you try to sell people what you think they need, you may not even do well. You may, in fact, go broke in the process. The problem with selling people what you think they need—even if they really need it—is that it takes too long and costs too much to educate them, i.e., to convince them that they need your product or service.

Probably to a more exaggerated extent than at any time in recorded history, people today demand instant gratification. Government policies over the past fifty years or more have convinced the average citizen he has a right to whatever he wants—and he has a right to it *now.* New cars, homes, vacations, flat-screen TVs, smart phones, iPads, and expensive, frivolous trinkets are now rights to the average person. If you try to buck this reality and insist on trying to sell people what you believe they need, you're hopelessly complicating the process of making money.

The simplest, safest approach to financial success is to be an accommodating free-enterpriser and make it a habit to sell people what they want.

The Thrill of Coercion

Anyone who bothers to read the newspaper cannot help but notice the never-ending proliferation of business regulation, fines, and imprisonment for white-collar types. It should be clear to all but the most naïve or uninformed individuals that one of the best ways to complicate your financial life is to become involved in an industry highly regulated by government bureaucrats (a.k.a. City Business Poachers, State Business Poachers, and Federal Business Poachers).

The government doesn't restrict itself to the excitement of frying Big Fish, either. It's true that when a Michael Milken comes along and has the gall to violate the most sacred of all federal laws—Thou Shalt Not Make Enormous Sums of Money—agency chiefs and prosecutors begin salivating and riling the masses by giving daily media interviews on the evils of wealth (until such time, of course, as they themselves receive lucrative offers to join one of the prestigious law firms who defend the "evil" people whom they are trying to prosecute). Today, however, everyone is fair game. All you need to do is attract attention, and the easiest way to do that is to be in a highly regulated business.

I used to jog occasionally with an attorney who had previously been a federal prosecutor, and I'll never forget him telling me, during an early morning jog, "Robert, you just can't imagine the thrill of having the full force of the federal government behind you. Coercing people becomes a way of life; it's addictive. All of us young prosecutors used to compare notes and joke about our most recent extortion triumphs. People either caved into our demands or lived to regret it. It was absolutely intoxicating."

Forget about whether you think it's fair. Right and wrong simply aren't relevant when it comes to government coercion. What I'm talking about here is reality. The important thing is to understand that if you want to simplify your pursuit of wealth, you should stay as far away from the Business Poachers as possible.

Knowing Your Principals

You can also save precious time, and simplify your life in the process, by being realistic about the principals with whom you deal. There are two kinds of principals, in particular, who can turn your business pursuits into living nightmares.

The first of these is the principal who is not highly motivated. It's tough enough to close a deal when all the parties involved are enthusiastic, but when motivation is low on the part of one or more of the key principals, complications are almost always close at hand. If a principal isn't motivated, the two most likely outcomes are: (1) He will ultimately back out of the deal, regardless of how many times he may have agreed to do it; or, (2) sensing that he's in the driver's seat, he will repeatedly attempt to negotiate a better deal for himself.

The second kind of principal that's a menace to simplicity is someone who doesn't have the final authority to make key decisions. If you're not talking directly with the guy who can say *yes* or *no*, it's wise to take everything, especially assurances, with a grain of salt. Better still, work on a different deal, one in which you have direct access to the decision-maker.

Cultivating the habit of being realistic about the principals with whom you deal is a huge step toward simplifying your deal-making pursuits.

Gaga Land

Finally, be careful about deals that are contingent upon some further major activity taking place, especially any kind of exotic financing, like the ever-elusive, mysterious "offshore funding," a phenomenon I never once saw materialize in all my years of deal-making. Contingencies have a remarkable way of never coming to fruition.

Nowhere is the primrose path of contingencies more crowded than in Gaga Land—also known as the world of real estate developers. If you're a real estate agent who has a commission at stake, it's always safest to assume that there is no second phase. Remember, tomorrow is a promissory note, but today is cash. **Real-World Rule No. 94: In the world of real estate developers, the second phase is something called** *bankruptcy.* Do yourself a favor and simplify your life by following the habit of steering clear of contingencies.

The Joy of Simplicity

There are more ways to complicate your life, both business and personal, than there are pages in this book, so the best overall guide I can give is to urge you to cultivate the habits of using common sense and not deluding yourself. Discard the notion, once and for all, that it's necessary to make things complex in order to make money.

Simplicity grants you a great deal of freedom, and freedom is perhaps the most gratifying result you can achieve. Take it from someone who was imprisoned by complexities throughout most of his early years in business. As I said at the outset of this chapter, if simplifying your life has been a problem for you, you're not alone. Virtually everyone possesses the problem to one degree or another, so you should resign yourself to the fact that it takes a lot of hard work.

It's worth repeating: It's the freest feeling in the world to rid yourself of projects and activities that clutter your life and contribute little or nothing to the achievement of your goals. You should be spending most of your time concentrating on constructive projects and activities that have the potential to make a real difference in the quality of your life.

To get where you want to be on the success ladder, in the shortest possible period of time, you should work at making the Simplicity Habit a central theme of your daily life.

CHAPTER 8

THE DRAIN PEOPLE ELIMINATION HABIT

Drain People are people who drain you of time, energy, peace of mind, relaxation, comfort, and/or money. Unfortunately, there are no statutes on the books outlawing the actions of Drain People. The only defense against them is for you to keep them, and/or get them, out of your life.

As a now-forgotten student of human nature once pointed out: You'll never smell like a rose if you roll in a dunghill. No matter what else you do right, if you associate with the wrong people, it's virtually impossible to succeed. In addition to causing endless complications, Drain People make you look bad in the eyes of others because of the generally accepted truth in the adage that "birds of a feather flock together." Who you associate with is like a neon sign that tells the world where you are on the success ladder at any given point in time.

Eliminating Drain People from your life can be a difficult task. One reason for this is that sidestepping a persistent Drain Person can cause significant discomfort. Another is that even when you know someone is a Drain Person, it's often tempting to make an exception for short-term profit. This is known as: Major Mistake. Trust me, you can't afford the long-term cost of the exception.

Finally, human beings have a tendency to give others the benefit of the doubt. People often make remarks such as, "But he means well." Maybe I'm dense, but I don't understand how to interpret "means well." I know what high blood pressure is. I know what a headache is. I know what aggravation is. But I'm not sure what "means well" is. Does it mean that someone should be allowed to rob you of your time, energy, and happiness because you believe his intentions are good?

You don't have enough hours in your life to give proper attention to the people whom you already know to be worthy, so why stretch your mental boundaries to find new ones? It's far better to trust your instincts and err on the side of caution. I find that with each passing year, my instincts about people continue to improve, and undoubtedly you've found the same to be true of yours. **Real-World Rule No. 155: The most prudent guideline to follow for judging potential Drain People is: When in doubt, keep them out.**

Lastly, don't make the often-fatal error of believing that a Drain Person will change, and certainly don't engage in any attempt to change him. People rarely, if ever, change. I recall one time in my business career when another party so offended me with his deceit and treachery in a business deal that I decided to strike him completely from my life, going to the extreme of cutting off all communication with him. I reasoned that if he could stoop to such a low level of integrity once, it must be such an ingrained part of his personality that he would not hesitate to do it again if the opportunity were to present itself.

To this terminally dishonest person's credit, he did send several letters of apology over the years. Finally, I relented and not only opened the lines of communication once more, but, over a period of time, began discussing a number of business proposals with him. The gory details of the story make me blush, so I'll get to the bottom line: After a brief period of time, he proved, as you've probably already guessed, that the first time around was no accident—that he was an individual who was capable of descending to incomprehensible levels of insincerity. Not only did he again display his lack of character at the moment of truth, but he even managed to outdo his earlier reprehensible deeds. This little anecdote may have reminded you of a similar experience from your own past, because most of us take the same classes (though not necessarily in the same order) during our enrollment in the University of Life.

What I've just described illustrates what I'm fond of referring to as the Law of the Scorpion, which is based on a tale you've probably heard before, but it's well worth repeating:

A scorpion sitting at the edge of a pond spots a frog. He asks the frog, "Hey, pal, how about giving me a lift to the other side of the pond? I can't swim."

The frog replies, "You've got to be kidding. No way I'm that dumb. I know what you guys are like. If I let you get on my back, you'll sting me, and I'll drown. Forget it."

The scorpion persists. "I can't believe how stupid you are. If I'm on your back, why in the world would I sting you when I can't swim? If you drown, I'll drown, too."

"Hmm, good point," reasons the frog. "Okay, get on."

The scorpion hops on the frog's back, and the frog takes off for the other side of the pond. About half way across, sure enough, the scorpion gives the frog a gigantic, poisonous sting in his back, and the two of them start to go under. With his last dying breath, the frog asks the scorpion, "Why in the heck did you do that? Now we're both going to drown."

To which the scorpion replies, with *his* last dying breath, "I couldn't help it. It's my nature."

Moral: Once a Drain Person, always a Drain Person; it's his nature. As an ancient proverb warns: You must have gold to make gold. Simplify your life by not deluding yourself into believing that a Drain Person will change. Once a person begins to drain you, cut your losses and get him completely out of your life. **Real-World Rule No. 42: Never leave the door open after a small evil manages to make its way inside, because only greater evils are waiting to gain**

entrance. Bad character is malignant; it grows and spreads if not checked early on.

Roll Call

Following are some examples of Drain People you've probably encountered at one time or another. An all-inclusive list could fill several volumes, but the sampling I present is more than adequate for our purposes. My objective is to jog your memory to perhaps bring to mind a Drain Person or two you may have unthinkingly allowed to slip into your life and remain there unchallenged. Even if the culprit doesn't fall into one of the categories below, hopefully my review will succeed in flushing him from your subconscious and into the open where you can more thoroughly and objectively examine him. If you aspire to great success, you absolutely must breed the habit of eliminating Drain People from your life.

The Burr Person

Professional speakers, in particular, are all too familiar with the Burr Person, the individual who since birth has had a burr firmly stuck in a sensitive part of his anatomy and acts accordingly. At speeches and seminars, he sits stiffly in his seat, arms folded in front of him, scowl chiseled on his face, and a sign rubber-stamped across his forehead that challenges the speaker: "Impress me."

Forget it, you can't. A Burr Person has already made up his mind ahead of time; the permanent implantation of his burr guarantees that. This is the kind of individual who subscribes to everything and orders every kind of direct-mail trinket imaginable. Then, after he has had sufficient time to read and use everything he ordered, he cancels all his subscriptions and returns all the adult mail-order toys he bought. But that's only the beginning.

Two days after cancelling the subscription or returning the merchandise, he begins contacting the Postmaster
General, the Federal Trade Commission, the local District
Attorney, the FBI, and the Commander of NATO, screaming to them that he has been defrauded, and demanding immediate justice. Even government bureaucrats don't take
him seriously, which is saying a lot. All the regulatory agencies have developed form letters for the Burr Person and routinely send copies to the appropriate parties as the complaints
roll in.

Burr People are everywhere, and they're particularly
recognizable for their lack of humor. Nothing irritates them
more than being around people who are happy or who are on a
motivational roll. I can recall one particular Burr Person from my
previous life who, listening to me excitedly describe how positive
I felt about the way things were going, glowered at me and said, in
an irritated voice, "I don't see why everything has to be positive.
What's *wrong* with being negative?" What a perfectly delightful
point of view.

Do your best to be humane to the Burr Person by maintaining
the habit of keeping your smiling face out of his sight so he can
be mad to his heart's content.

The Changer

The Changer doesn't deal in money; he deals in (attempted)
people change. Specifically, he wants to change you. The
Changer cannot be happy unless he is successful in converting
you to conform to his ways. While continually chastising you for
not changing, it never occurs to him that you may not want to
change, that you actually like your life just fine the way it is. And
certainly it never crosses his mind that you might find *his* way of
life to be deplorable.

The Chiseler

The Chiseler is a world-class drainer. In fact, he counts on wearing you down so he eventually can get his way. Nothing can be smooth or simple with him. The Chiseler always has to get a better deal, an extra bonus, a larger cut. But the ultimate is when it comes time for him to write you a check. Never mind that he owes you the money, he practically makes you beg for it. There's a bit of sadism in every world-class Chiseler.

Unless you're a fellow chiseler who enjoys a good chisel match now and then with one of your own kind, the Chiseler is truly repugnant. He's really nothing more than a scorpion in a business suit. It's simply not possible for him to change; it's his nature.

The Conditional Person

The Conditional Person roams the earth bearing strings-attached gifts for the unwary. His game is entrapment. He needs to give to others so he can turn around and pounce on his prey, demanding (usually in subtle ways) to extract a psychological price equal to what he perceives to be the value of his gift—plus, of course, 385 percent compounded interest. Nothing makes a Conditional Person happier than bumping into a naive taker. Beware of Conditional People bearing gifts of incense and myrrh, especially if they want you to sign a promissory note.

The Deal Gabber

Did you ever talk to someone about a deal and be delighted to find that he's very excited about it, often so excited that he urges you to overnight the pertinent information to him? Then, when you do as he requests, an amazing thing happens: nothing. After not hearing from him for two days, you call his office, only to find that he's on vacation for two weeks and that he left on the very day he told you to overnight the material to him. So why did he urge you to send the information to him overnight? Nothing mysterious about it: Deal Gabbers simply love to gab.

Every phase of one's life must ultimately come to an end, and so it was that after 11,287 Deal Gabber experiences, the Deal Gabber phase of my life ended with an all-time, super-duper Deal Gabber episode. After discussing a certain deal with a (then unknown to me) Deal Gabber named Charles, and taking great pains to qualify his degree of interest, he asked me to send the pertinent information to him by Federal Express. He pointed out that since it was Friday, I should send it to his home for Saturday delivery because he was leaving town on Monday.

He said he then would be able to read it on Saturday and call me at home Saturday night. He emphasized he would be home all day Saturday and Saturday evening, so there was no doubt in my mind he was serious. Further, since his Monday trip happened to be to my city, and he would be staying at a hotel near my office, he said he would call when he arrived and set up an appointment so we could get down to specifics.

As you would expect of any good trooper, I worked several hours putting together a beautiful package that would have made Picasso proud, then hustled to beat the Fed Ex cutoff at 6 p.m. Being an anti-pennywise, dollar-foolish thinker by nature, I figured the extra $10 or so for Saturday delivery was a paltry sum to pay to get the deal into high gear before Charles left town.

Having not heard from him by Saturday evening, I thought I had better call just to make sure he received the package. No luck—answering machine. When I didn't hear from him by Sunday afternoon, I called again, and again got an answering machine—and, of course, no return call. Ditto, Sunday evening. Because I'm sure you've been there many times yourself, you've undoubtedly already guessed that not only did I not hear from him that weekend, or while he was staying at a hotel near my office on Monday and Tuesday, I never heard from him at all—i.e., as in *never again*.

Real-World Rule No. 251: Proceed with caution when someone with whom you've had no experience enthusiastically tells you, "It

sounds great. Why don't you overnight the material to me?" If he's a Deal Gabber, the translation is, "I don't have the courage to tell you I'm not interested, so I'll just humor you by asking you to send the material overnight."

While all Deal Gabbers clearly love to employ the rush-rush routine, sometimes their need to gab is so uncontrollable that they would rather continue talking to you than pull a disappearing act. One of the most cherished ploys of a bona-fide Deal Gabber is to talk endlessly about the multi-million-dollar deals he's working on—$5 million he recently invested in this, $10 million he recently invested in that—but when it comes to the paltry $50,000 you need for your deal, he regretfully has to pass on the opportunity. Why? Because he's "all invested up right now," or he's "having a problem that he has to get cleared up first," or he's "in the middle of an expensive lawsuit." The script is always the same: "If only you had contacted me just a week earlier, I could have done the deal with no problem." Sound familiar?

People often drive themselves crazy trying to figure out why a Deal Gabber talks . . . and talks . . . and talks . . . then fails to act. But the reality is that it's not all that complicated. A Deal Gabber rarely has ill intent; he just likes to hear the sound of his voice. He simply loves to gab. It's his mission in life, the central joy of his world of delusions. Don't waste your energy getting mad at a Deal Gabber; just make it a habit never to talk business with him again.

The Desperate Person

The Desperate Person is perhaps the most dangerous of all Drain People, because he's prone to stretching his moral beliefs. Also, a Desperate Person panics easily, making ill-advised decisions that can bring you down with him. Worst of all, because he feels he has nothing to lose, the Desperate Person is a potential lethal weapon. He can afford to try anything. When the Desperate Person reaches the frantic stage, make certain you aren't close enough to be injured by his bad judgment.

The Destroyer
The Destroyer's objective is to tear you down, preferably by assuring you that you can't succeed at what you're trying to accomplish. If there's one thing you don't need in your life, it's someone who emphasizes negatives and tries to chip away at your confidence. Unfortunately, we live in a very negative world, and we don't have to look very far to find someone who is happy to tell us why our objectives are unattainable.

Most Destroyers are just unhappy people who continually confirm the truth of the misery-loves-company axiom. It can be like getting caught in a spider's web, because the unhappy Destroyer thrives on the opportunity to pull others down to his level. If you're not careful, such a Destroyer will soon have you prostrating yourself and relating your troubles to him. And when that happens, he will happily pontificate to you, volunteer to become your psychologist, and tell you everything that's wrong with you—with a certitude that implies that he is problem free and totally well adjusted. His ultimate joy is to succeed in making *you* psychologically dependent upon *him.*

Another kind of Destroyer is the expert, a narrow-minded creature who drips conventional wisdom from the corners of his permanently opened mouth. Loaded to the gills with an abundance of wisdom, he feels compelled to tear you down. The Business World Arena, in particular, is saturated with self-appointed experts whose chief objective seems to be to make certain that you clearly understand their superiority over you.

You should nurture the habit of not allowing yourself to be intimidated by experts offering conventional wisdom. In truth, conventional wisdom is nothing more than a proclamation of unknown origin stating that something can't be done, until someone too dumb to understand the proclamation comes along and does it, after which time whatever he does then becomes the new conventional wisdom.

To paraphrase Viktor Frankl, an expert is nothing more than a person who no longer sees the forest of truth for the trees of facts. If you want to make the expert—or any Destroyer, for that matter—mad, just prove him wrong. Better still, if you want to improve your chances of achieving positive results, you should practice the habit of completely eliminating him from your life.

The Hallucinator

The Hallucinator usually is just a Desperate Person waiting to happen. His self-delusions are so extreme that they take him beyond a waking dream state into a completely different dimension.

I recall visiting a financial newsletter writer in the early Eighties whom I had always suspected of being a Hallucinator, but I hadn't known him well enough to be certain. He had achieved a degree of publicity for his doom-and-gloom forecasts, and, as a result, the hallucinatory cells in his brain had begun flexing their muscles. During the course of our conversation, he gazed upward and, in a matter-of-fact tone, said, "I recently had a vision that I'm going to be president of the United States."

Thinking he was joshing me, I replied, tongue in cheek, "Great, but are you sure you want the job?"

He then looked straight at me, eyes glazed over like someone who had just returned from a ride in a spaceship, and replied, "It's already a fait accompli. The vision is clear; the wheels of history are in place. I couldn't stop it now, even if I wanted to."

I was about to chuckle and one-up him with another humorous retort, but my mouth froze closed when I saw the faraway gaze in his eyes. Again, he looked upward with a blank stare, whereupon I began sizing up the distance between me and the door. "Hey," I thought to myself in horror, "this guy is serious. He really believes he's going to be president!" Forget the fact that he had more skeletons in his closet than Forest Lawn. His notion of reality was that he was going to be president—period.

The Sufi poet Jalaluddin Rumi once wrote that even Jesus fled from the fool, saying, "I can make the blind see, the deaf hear, the lame run and raise the dead, but I cannot turn the fool away from his folly." That being the case, you'd be wise to make it a habit to keep your distance from Hallucinators.

The Liar

Remember the definition of honesty: the absolute refusal to lie, steal, cheat, or deceive in any way. I already discussed this in some detail in Chapter 5, particularly as it relates to various types of lying, so we needn't look at more examples. What's important here is to emphasize that you have a right—some might argue an obligation—to hold others in your life to the same high standards to which you adhere.

Also, I can't emphasize enough how easy it is to delude yourself in this area. You must get in the habit of observing what people do, not just what they say. This gets back to the problem of going overboard to give people the benefit of the doubt. While it may seem like a noble gesture, it's even more noble to focus your energy on people who consistently demonstrate their honesty, who don't need the benefit of the doubt. Good rule to follow: When in doubt, keep the person out . . . of your life.

The Rude Monger

The Rude Monger is totally self-centered. He rarely, if ever, says *please* or *thank you*; he is almost always late for meetings; he regularly interrupts telephone conversations, asking the party on the other end of the line to excuse him while he carries on a discussion with someone in his office; he is curt, insensitive, and discourteous; and, above all, he's a master at not returning phone calls and not calling people back when he says he will. Obviously, a Deal Gabber may also qualify as a Rude Monger.

The Rude Monger's usual excuse (following a profuse and flowery apology) for not returning your call is that he has been super busy and just hasn't had time. Because of his self-centered psyche, he doesn't realize that this is a double insult. First, by telling you how busy he's been, he is clearly implying that you *aren't* busy. Personally, I think people who dwell on how busy they are sound like amateurs. In the real world, I assume that everyone with whom I deal is busy. Second, "haven't had time" implies that you're a low priority on his list, and your chances of getting results with someone who sees you as a low priority are very slim.

Perhaps the most pragmatic reason for staunchly maintaining the habit of keeping the Rude Monger out of your life is that it's inefficient for you to deal with him. If you're properly focused on success, the one thing you don't have time to hear is how busy the other guy is. You should be far more concerned about how busy *you* are, because, unbeknownst to the Rude Monger, you probably have a lot less time for him than he has for you. In that light, it also becomes a matter of self-respect, because a person who doesn't value his time doesn't value himself.

The Skinflint

The Skinflint is a first cousin to the Chiseler, but with less intelligence. Though he isn't capable of seeing it, he constantly loses out because of his obsession for acting in pennywise, dollar-foolish ways.

Awhile back, a fellow speaker called me about a book he had been working on that he was convinced would be a blockbuster bestseller. (Note: To put this in proper perspective, you must understand that *every* speaker is always working on a book that he is convinced will be a blockbuster bestseller—if he could just get it published.) He was aware of my experience both with publishing my own books and working with other publishers and wanted to know if I would be willing to meet with him and give him some advice. Because we had a mutual friend, I agreed to do so, but told him I would have to check my calendar and get back to him.

Before getting off the phone, he mentioned that a few years ago he had written a self-published paperback booklet about the physical and logistical aspects of putting on seminars. During the course of my career, I, like every other writer and speaker I know of, have given away thousands of complimentary copies of my books and audio tapes, not only to friends and acquaintances, but as goodwill business gestures. Therefore, I didn't give it a second thought when I told this speaker that I really would love to receive a copy of his booklet.

As the cliché goes, there's a first time for everything. The slim little paperback arrived in the mail a few days later, *with a bill enclosed.* The bill included $9.95 for the book, plus $3.00 for postage and handling! My first instinct was to chuckle. The pennywise, dollar-foolish message was clear: "You pay me full price for my paperback booklet, including postage and handling, then give me whatever book-publishing information I need from you for free." If this Skinflint had charged me only for his book, maybe it would have qualified only as a run-of-the-mill, humorous Skinflint story. But postage and handling? We're talking legendary pennywise, dollar-foolish material here.

The Skinflint also displays a remarkable talent for feigning a grab for the dinner check, missing it, faking a cough, and turning his head away. Then, just as you reflexively move your hand toward the check, he immediately says something like, "Are you sure?" This is followed very quickly by, "Well, okay. It's very gracious of you. Next time around it will be my treat." Sure, and Vladimir Putin will be starting at second base for the Reds next season. As with the Chiseler, the Skinflint can't help himself. It's a psychological disease; he's incapable of changing.

Legalman

Finally, we get to the perpetual World Heavyweight Drain Champion, Legalman—also commonly referred to as "attorney," "lawyer," and by a variety of obscenities. Legalman is that omnipresent humanoid commonly perceived to be the answer to the majority of people's problems, both real and imagined. Given that he has a permanent hold on the top ranking, I've reserved him a generous amount of space befitting his elevated status.

Years ago, my hobby was supporting Legalman in regal style. I flew him around the country first class, put him up in the finest hotels, and took him to the most elegant restaurants. I used to spend endless hours with him, joking and laughing, talking sports, philosophizing, and, yes, sometimes even discussing legal matters.

One Saturday, Legalman, my accountant, and I were having a summit meeting in my office with a centimillionaire, Mr. Vulchar, regarding a deal I was trying to put together. At one point, Mr. Vulchar, who was reviewing my financial statements, looked up and said to me, "Your legal and accounting fees are higher than mine. Why in the world do you need this much legal and accounting work?"

Embarrassed, I mumbled some incoherent, inaudible excuse, after which Mr. Vulchar waved his right hand in the direction of Legalman and my accountant and bellowed, "These guys don't work for you; you work for them. You're a slave to these characters."

We never did put the deal together, but Mr. Vulchar's blunt observation festered inside me until I finally decided to do something about it. It took years to break my expensive addiction to Legalman, but eventually I succeeded. At the time of Mr. Vulchar's observation about my being a slave to Legalman and my accountant, my legal bills were averaging about $6,000 a month. For many years now, by contrast, my *annual* legal expenses have been virtually zero. What I finally realized is that the need to use Legalman is, for the most part, a figment of a deluded public's collective imagination.

If you implement only one piece of advice I offer in this chapter, it should be this: Make it a habit to avoid like the plague legal entanglements of any kind, especially lawsuits. There are very few things in life as frustrating as being a party to a lawsuit and having to witness a bunch of shamelessly unprepared attorneys fake their way through years of litigation, while simultaneously doing their best to prolong it.

Rarely does either side come out ahead in a lawsuit. You either lose the case and lose to your attorney (i.e., in legal fees), which means you lose big; or you win the case and *still lose to your attorney*, which in most instances means you sustain an overall loss. Remember, your loss not only must be measured in dollars, but time—time spent in court, time answering interrogatories, time meeting with Legalman, time having your deposition taken, and on a wide variety of other obscene "legal" activities.

Master of Intimidation

First and foremost, Legalman is *the* master intimidator. Now, understand that I'm not referring only to the other guy's attorney. On the contrary, it's your attorney with whom you should be primarily concerned. Easily intimidated folks simply can't comprehend that it's their own attorney from whom they most need protection. Your attorney is the one who poses the greatest threat to your solvency and who will kill more deals for you during your lifetime than all your opponents' attorneys combined.

One of Legalman's best intimidation props is "The Certificate," which is usually prominently displayed on the wall just behind him, ideally about six inches above his head for easy client viewing. The Certificate is commonly referred to in street parlance as *law degree* and is absolutely awesome to most clients. Little wonder. After all, none other than the United States government stands squarely behind The Certificate. That framed little piece of paper on Legalman's wall is a written confirmation that he is entitled to all the rights and privileges of the government-mandated legal monopoly in this country.

And an amazing monopoly it is. Attorneys are attorneys; prosecutors are attorneys; judges are attorneys; and over half of all U.S. congressmen are attorneys. This means that Legalman makes the law, argues the law, and interprets the law. If ever there was a fix, this is it.

Legalman also tries to intimidate his prey by displaying an air of superior intelligence. He takes great pleasure in perpetuating this ruse by dispensing an overdose of Legalese. If you're unfamiliar with the term *Legalese*, it's a language taught in law school, the unspoken purpose of which is to thoroughly confuse clients (on both sides) and thereby put Legalman in a position to call the shots more easily. After all, how can a client argue with Legalman's logic if he has no idea what he's talking about?

If Legalman didn't inundate you with an endless stream of wherefores, whereofs, and whereases, you might start to get the idea that The Certificate is just a cover for a rather easy job. This might cause you to no longer be in awe of him, which in turn might lead you to conclude that you don't need him at all. And that's something Legalman just isn't going to allow to happen if there's any way he can help it. No matter how badly he may fail in other areas, he's acutely aware that, at all costs, he must succeed in intimidating you. His very livelihood—and, just as important, his ego—depend upon it.

With all due respect, my own experience with Legalman has convinced me that, by and large, he not only is not particularly bright, but is incredibly lazy as well. (Why work hard if you're protected by monopoly laws?) This laziness tends to manifest itself as gross negligence. Legalman will be happy to talk Legalese with you all day long, but just try to get him to shut up, sit down, roll up his sleeves, and actually draft a document. Fat chance. He'll think of every excuse this side of Harvard to avoid putting pen to paper, which is why most cases are settled out of court, many on the courthouse steps the day the trial is scheduled to commence. It's a rare occasion when Legalman is prepared to go to trial. He'd always rather settle than fight, provided, of course, that he's milked the case for all it's worth and has run out of stalling tactics.

The Finely Honed Art

There basically are two kinds of attorneys who kill deals: those who admit it (none) and those who deny it (all).

Many of us take Legalman's deal-killing prowess for granted, but it's a finely honed art that takes years to master. It's not as easy as it was in the good old days, when all Legalman had to do was dash into the closing at the final moment and shred the deal into legal confetti without so much as working up a sweat. Today, he has to be much more sophisticated and subtle about his intentions. He must pretend as though he actually wants the deal to close. A naive person might be inclined to ask, "Why in the world would Legalman not want a deal to close in the first place?" There are many reasons for his deal-killing antics, and all are bad from the client's viewpoint.

Two of the more common ones are:

First, learned instincts. An attorney who graduated at the top of his class at Stanford Law School once told me that his legal education consisted solely of learning how to find problems. Not solve them—*find* them. In other words, Legalman usually isn't as malevolent as he may seem. It's just that deal-killing is the only thing he's been trained to do.

Second, jealousy. This ties in with Legalman's belief that he possesses innate, superior intelligence, as well as a better formal education than you or me. It therefore stands to reason that he not only has the ability to make better legal judgments than his clients, but business judgments as well. Thus, Legalman uses one of his best intimidation ploys as a weapon to kill your deal. Often, he does this under the guise of renegotiating the terms of the deal, which can always be counted on as a surefire deal-killer. Shame on you if you allow this to occur, because you should never give Legalman the opportunity to be in a position to negotiate the terms of your deal in the first place, let alone renegotiate them.

No doubt Legalman would love to be a businessman, but, in truth, he doesn't have the entrepreneurial courage to come out from behind The Certificate that hangs on his wall. That's why it eats away at him when he occasionally has a client who makes more money in one good closing than he makes in a whole year of client-mooching.

One time, loud and clear, so there's no miscommunication on this point: Never ask Legalman for business advice! If he volunteers it (which he will, usually in subtle ways), there's no need to raise your voice. Just reach into your breast pocket, pull out your scissors (always carry a pair of scissors with you when meeting with Legalman), reach across his desk, and cut off his tie exactly two-and-a-half inches below the knot. He'll get the point. Trust me.

And, remember, it's up to you to cultivate the habit of differentiating between legal and business decisions before you can be in a position to know when to muzzle Legalman.

Fee-building Treachery
When it comes to fee-building, never delude yourself about Legalman's inherent conflict of interest: The quicker a deal closes or a matter is disposed of, the less income he makes. It's one of those inescapable realities of life. Following are a handful of Legalman's more shameful fee-building tactics, tactics for which you must always be on the alert.

The Chat

This is perhaps Legalman's favorite day-to-day fee-builder. Providing you're a client who pays his bills on time, Legalman will be more than happy to chat with you on the phone about anything you desire: the Super Bowl, the latest Steven Spielberg movie, how dumb some other client's attorney is, or, if there's nothing more interesting to chat about, a good old-fashioned joke will do. When it comes to fee-building, clients consistently make the mistake of falling into this trap. It's imperative to remember that talk is *not* cheap. It is, in fact, very expensive when talking to Legalman. **Real-World Rule No. 31: Don't call Legalman to chat. Legalman doesn't chat; he bills.**

The Research Project

This is another problem that stems from your being careless in your conversations with Legalman. One of his favorite tricks is to make a research project out of an innocent question on your part, which means delegating work to a young legal flunky in his office. Legalman loves a good research project, even if the client doesn't specifically ask for one, because it's a great way of leveraging himself (which is a nice way of saying he can continue to evade doing any work, while making money through the efforts of an underling).

Worse, many so-called research projects turn out to be nothing more than copying scams. A number of years ago, I asked Legalman a casual question about the legal structure of a certain type of corporation. He said he wasn't certain about the answer, but would check it out. We exchanged comments about mutual friends, travel, and other trivia for another ten or fifteen minutes, then said our goodbyes. Surprise! A couple of weeks later I received a huge envelope that contained about a hundred copies of pages from a variety of law books, journals, and magazines, with a cover letter explaining that one of Legalman's assistants had "researched" my question thoroughly and that he hoped the enclosed material would satisfy my inquiry. I was (naively) dumfounded. Even if he had sent the material free of charge, there was no way I was going to sit down and read a hundred pages of Legalese. But it wasn't free. A $6,000 bill followed the package two weeks later.

It's crucial to your wallet that you develop the habit of making it clear to Legalman that you aren't interested in his doing a lot of elaborate research on your behalf.

The Meeting

Legalman also loves meetings. It's easier than holding a phone receiver to his ear, he can show off the fancy offices you helped pay for, and he can pontificate Legalese to his heart's content. Best of all, he doesn't have to do any drafting (i.e., work). And if the meeting involves parties from the other side of a transaction, remember that all the irrelevant chit-chat that Legalman and the other side's attorney engage in—about their upcoming Sunday golf match, for example—is going to be paid for by you.

Lastly, be sure to practice the habit of challenging Legalman's bills. Legalman has an annoying habit of seeing a regular client as an annuity. Work or not, he just assumes he has the right to bill well-paying clients each month.

The Triple-bypass Legaldectomy

Legalman's methodology is based on a surgical procedure developed by a legendary attorney named I. Stickitoohymn, Esq. The operation is called a Triple-bypass Legaldectomy, and Legalman has been in Sir Stickitoohymn's debt ever since he first developed this operation centuries ago. If you've never undergone this delicate surgical procedure, I can best describe it as the pain you might expect to experience if you were to submit to simultaneous root-canal work and a hemorrhoid operation.

In a Triple-bypass Legaldectomy, Legalman (1) intimidates his client, (2) kills his client's deal, and (3) removes a malignant growth of money from his client's bank account. In really extreme cases, Legalman may manage to remove *all* money from his client's bank account—malignant, benign, or otherwise. If you find it unavoidable to engage the services of Legalman, be sure to check your cash reserves. You're going to need them if his prognosis calls for a Triple-bypass Legaldectomy.

In wrapping up Legalman (interesting choice of words), I want to make it absolutely clear that nothing I've said here should be taken as a blanket indictment of Legalman. On the contrary, even though the late Chief Justice Warren E. Burger stated that he believed lawyers generally overcharge their clients and that law schools and bar associations neglect professional ethics, an innate sense of fairness compels me to point out that it's really only about 97 percent of the attorneys in America who are lazy, incompetent, negligent, and greedy—yet they make a bad name for the entire profession. In fact, some of my best friends are . . . well, on second thought, strike that. Just concentrate on nurturing the habit of keeping Legalman out of your life to the greatest extent possible.

Just Doing What They're Supposed To Do

The list of Drain People goes on and on: the Complainer, the Finger Pointer, the Guilt Monger, the Irrationalist, the Sadist, the Self-righteous, the Silver Tongue, the Territorial Person, the Thin Skinned, and many, many more. What all Drain People have in common is that they drain you of time, energy, peace of mind, relaxation, comfort, and/or money.

Interpersonal conflicts waste time and energy, and Drain People are masters at causing interpersonal conflicts. The bottom line is that Drain People are simply a drain. If you allow Drain People to remain in your life, your mind will be cluttered with negative emotions, which hinders your ability to concentrate on worthy people, those who have the potential to add value to your life and you to theirs.

Finally, don't drive yourself crazy trying to figure out why a Drain Person acts the way he does. To again paraphrase Jim Rohn, liars are supposed to lie; cheaters are supposed to cheat; complainers are supposed to complain. Unless you've decided to open a Drain People Rehabilitation Center, or are a psychiatrist getting paid for your analyses, forget the *why*. Once and for all: Drain People are *supposed* to drain. It's their life's work. It's what they live for. Don't question it; just concentrate on religiously practicing the Drain People Elimination Habit. It's a habit about which you have to be ever vigilant, because if you become lax, you run the danger of allowing that one Drain Person into your life who might cause a major, irreversible problem that could shatter everything you've worked to achieve.

CHAPTER 9

THE SELF-DISCIPLINE HABIT

"B e first the master of yourself, and only then a master of others," advised Baltasar Gracian. Mastering yourself is not the easiest of tasks, because within each of us exists a perpetual struggle between our intellect and our emotions. That's what self-disciplinc is all about—overriding your instinctive desire for instant gratification and acting instead on your intellectual conclusions. A truly self-disciplined individual is able to do this even when his emotions are running high.

Self-discipline manifests itself as a feeling of self-control. Contrary to the pop-psych preachings of our modern era, freedom does not come from "letting it all hang out" or taking a devil-may-care attitude. Freedom comes from triumphing over your emotions and proving to yourself that you can be master of your destiny. When you allow your emotions to rule, you subject yourself to emotional enslavement, and never is a person less free than when he is enslaved by his emotions.

My discussion of the Present Living Habit in Chapter 4 is not intended to imply that you should totally ignore the future. My emphasis in that chapter is on striving *toward* future goals by working at something that adds meaning to your life. However, living in the present does not mean that you should take any action that happens to make you feel good today without regard to tomorrow's consequences.

Understanding that our emotions tend to be oriented toward immediate gratification is an essential first step toward developing the Self-Discipline Habit. Unfortunately, the Natural Law of Balance assures us that those things that provide the greatest amount of immediate pleasure usually are the very things that are most detrimental to our long-term health, happiness, and success. It's important to distinguish between the immediate, day-to-day enjoyment to be found in doing one's work—in having a meaningful life—and in trying to enjoy the fruits of one's labor before they have been earned.

Future-oriented Thinking

What I'm talking about here is future-oriented thinking—connecting today's actions with tomorrow's results. No matter how much you enjoy living in the present, prudence dictates that you take the future into consideration. Don't make the mistake of thinking of the long term as some vague point in time that will never make its appearance. It will, and almost always sooner than you anticipate. As I pointed out in Chapter 4, the future has an annoying habit of arriving ahead of schedule.

Again, it's a matter of developing a correct perception of reality, and, as discussed earlier, that's something that requires knowledge and wisdom. So long as you have a reasonable storehouse of knowledge and wisdom, the one excuse for doing the wrong thing that is never valid is, "I didn't have a choice; I had to do it."

This "nonexcuse excuse" is used repeatedly by people who continually fail. They refuse to admit to themselves that it is within their power *not* to do the wrong thing if their intellect tells them that the long-term consequences are likely to be destructive. The alternative is to pay the short-term price of immediate discomfort in exchange for enjoying greater rewards over the long term.

It's worth repeating: You *always* have a choice. For example, an individual who has not developed the Self-Discipline Habit may repeatedly yield to the temptation to do business with someone who has caused him problems in the past. The consequences of such a mistake are often great enough to have a major bearing on an individual's success or failure over the long term.

The person who succeeds and the person who fails at the same endeavor may both know how to succeed, but often there is one major difference between them: The successful individual disciplines himself to do the right thing, while the unsuccessful individual allows his emotions to prevail. Charles DeGaulle admitted to his weakness in this area when he said, "I'm often wrong in what I do, but rarely wrong in what I predict."

As with all habits, self-discipline is a learned art, and to master this art requires two basic steps: First, you must consistently analyze the probable, long-term consequences of your actions. Second, you must be tenacious in *acting* in accordance with what you have determined to be in your long-term best interest.

Cracked Mousse

A good example of implementing these two steps is reflected in an experience of mine back in 1984. The producer of *ABC News Nightline* called me and said he would like to do a show on "fear in the workplace." He had lined up Harold Geneen, former chairman of IT&T, and a psychiatrist from Wharton to be two of the guests, and said that because my name was synonymous with intimidation, he felt I would be the ideal third guest. Shades of the old days!

I told him that even though I admired Ted Koppel and thought it would be interesting to do the show, it probably would be unfair to him. I explained that *Winning Through Intimidation* had been badly miscast by the media, and that it was not a book about how to get ahead by intimidating others. The producer assured me that he understood and again urged me to do the show. Finally, I agreed to do it, but warned him that I had given up playing the intimidation clown years ago, and that Koppel may be less than thrilled with my answers. Again he assured me that he fully understood, and the deal was on.

Notwithstanding the producer's assurances, however, Koppel's opening question to me was, "Mr. Ringer, you've been called 'the Apostle of Intimidation.' How do you feel about motivating workers through fear?"

Sound the trumpets, the moment had arrived. I had taken the trouble to analyze the long-term consequences of my actions before coming to the studio, and I was determined to follow through and act in what I had concluded to be my long-term best interests. I fully recognized that it *was* within my power to demonstrate self-discipline and say what I really felt, rather than going along with the producer's hoped-for, three-ring-circus show as I had done so many times earlier in my career.

In a serious, calm tone, I said to Koppel, "Well, Ted, first of all I have to take exception to the label 'Apostle of Intimidation.'" Koppel twitched, his hair mousse cracked, and the interview went downhill from there. As you might have guessed, the program was a dud. Though I felt badly for the producer, I had warned him that I would not go along with playing the bad guy in an extemporaneous intimidation skit, and he had assured me that the show was not going to go in that direction.

The moral is that just because you've failed to exercise good sense and self-discipline in the past (as I had with *Time* magazine and the rest of the media earlier in my career) doesn't mean you have to continue to do so. Remember: It's *always* within your power to act in your long-term best interests.

Conquering the Impulsive Urge

People generally fall into one of two groups when it comes to the basis of their actions. Individuals tend either to act on impulse or they employ self-discipline to guide their actions, and it's pretty obvious which type of individual tends to succeed and which type tends to fail. Acting impulsively—in knee-jerk-response fashion—to what is going on around you equates to an out-of-control and dangerous life. Nonetheless, we are continually tempted to act impulsively, and impulsive action is based on emotion rather than intellect or common sense.

Immunity Not Granted

In the marketplace, as untold millions have discovered, the consequences of acting impulsively by joining the actions of the crowd can be catastrophic. The so-called lemming effect (one person following another over the edge of a financial cliff) has fascinated students of human nature for centuries. The condition of your Self-Discipline Habit is severely tested when the crowd is heading in one direction, and your intellect and/or common sense tells you that it's the wrong direction.

That's when you must exercise the self-discipline to override the momentary comfort of being in the mainstream. When you're tempted to act impulsively in a situation like this, remind yourself that the mainstream generally doesn't do very well over the long term. Civilization progresses as a result of the actions of a handful of great minds. Mainstream people then simply go along for the ride—and usually too late, at that.

In Chapter 1, I mentioned the sad tale of famous real estate guru, but he certainly was not alone in his overzealousness toward real estate. He just happened to be a highly visible victim of the madness-of-the-real-estate-crowd syndrome. The worst epidemic of the so-called boom mentality in real estate in the 1980s took place just south of the U.S. border, in a large, unruly nation known as *Texas*. In the late 1970s and early 1980s, I recall telling acquaintances in Texas that perhaps they should scale back their building activities, since the rest of the country was coming apart at the seams.

But scaling back was unthinkable them. The only question was whether Texas real estate developers would laugh or get mad at me for daring to say such preposterous things. The typical response was something to the effect of, "Oh, recessions don't happen in Texas. We're pretty much immune. It's a whole different ball game here." Thanks to this kind of self-delusive attitude, the bankruptcy courts in this "immune" area of North America stayed quite busy throughout the 1980s. If you're not a famous heart surgeon, a former Secretary of the Treasury, or a once-skyrocketing billionaire, you didn't even rate a second glance on the Texas bankruptcy court dockets back then.

As always, as the real estate boom heats up again—and you can be sure it will—those who have the self-discipline to get out long before the next bubble bursts will be the ones who come out ahead.

A Dangerous Arena for Impulsive Souls

An individual is particularly susceptible to impulsive action in the heat of negotiating situations. If a person becomes involved in high-level negotiations without first having cultivated the Self-Discipline Habit, he's likely to end up looking like he had a run-in with a drug cartel operative. I know, because I have the scars to prove it.

Beware "Too Good to Be True"

You have to be careful not to give a knee-jerk *yes* when someone makes a satisfactory counteroffer, or, worse, a counteroffer that seems too good to be true. Almost without fail, the instinct that tells you something sounds too good to be true turns out to be correct. Unfortunately, if you make the mistake of being too fast on the *yes*, the realities usually don't dawn on you until hours after the meeting ends. You're driving on the freeway, smiling contently, and all at once it hits you—the key point you failed to take into consideration when you impulsively agreed to that too-good-to-be-true counteroffer. You suddenly realize that you either have to take a financial bloodbath or compromise your moral standards by backing out of a deal to which you have already agreed.

The best defense against making this kind of mistake is to set a firm policy that you won't agree to any offer—no matter how good it sounds—before calling time-out and carefully analyzing it in private. Preferably, you should at least think about overnight. If you can't get that much time, try to get a few hours. And if that's not feasible, ask for fifteen minutes. Anything is better than a knee-jerk *yes*, so the important thing is to maintain the self-discipline to ask for as much time as you can get.

A Clever Thing to Say

Good listening not only promotes good human relations, it's also pragmatic. Will Durant, after spending seventy years researching and writing about world civilizations, concluded, "Nothing is often a good thing to do, and almost always a clever thing to say." Heeding Durant's advice, I've tried hard over the years to repress my impulse to jump in and talk at the first sign of an opening. Particularly when negotiating, I've disciplined myself to let the other guy talk . . . and talk . . . and talk, while I listen . . . listen . . . listen.

I recall being on the other side of the table in a negotiating situation when the other party made the mistake of talking when he should have been listening. During a final negotiating session, I started to list the terms I would accept, and after stating that I wanted "A," "B," and "C," he suddenly interrupted me and said, "I know, I know—and you want 'D,' 'E,' and 'F.'" To my surprise, he had rattled off what he thought were the figures I was about to ask for. He was wrong. The figures he stated were much *higher* than those I was going to ask for. Trying to mask my excitement, I quickly said, "Right! Right! We're completely in tune. How did you ever guess? That's exactly what I was going to say!"

Sure enough, those were the precise terms upon which we closed the deal. The other party's little error—not having the self-discipline to hear me out before talking—ended up costing him an additional $180,000. That's about $16,000 per word! A very high price to pay for not developing the habit of controlling your urge to speak too soon.

Trump Cards and Greed

Here's one for graduate students only: Nurture the self-discipline to head off the impulse to cavalierly throw out trump cards when negotiating. The purpose of trump cards is to trump, so always hold back a couple of cards for the finale. Almost without fail, you'll need to call on one or more of them as the going gets tough in the closing stages. The wise negotiator always keeps something in reserve because experience has taught him that there's no such thing as a smooth closing. He knows he's going to need a trump card or two when the inevitable renegotiation process begins. Yes, I said *re*negotiation.

Also, if you're careless about using your trump cards, you open yourself to the Human Greed Factor, which works like so: If you suggest the possibility of doing "X," providing the other party will go along with "Y," often the other party will reject "Y," but insist that "X" be part of the deal. It's dirty pool, to be sure, but sharp negotiators have been using this cute little tactic since Cro-Magnon man first appeared on Earth. All other things being equal, you're better off to save "X" as a trump card, to be used near the finish line when a concession is needed to get the deal closed. **Real-World Rule No. 168: Any time you introduce a compromise chip into a negotiation, it has a mysterious way of becoming a firm part of the deal in the other party's mind.**

Also, recognize that one of the best ways to hoard trump cards is to yield on as many nonessential points as possible. It's a matter of controlling the impulse to reject a point just because you feel it's inequitable. The results-oriented question is not whether or not something is equitable. A far more important question is: How much does it really matter? In fact, you should be anxious to yield on as many nonessential points as possible, because the more times you give in, the easier it is to get the other side to concede on those points that *are* essential to you.

In the heat of negotiations, don't allow false pride to interfere when it comes to yielding on nonessential points. Remember, self-discipline is a matter of intellect overruling emotions. Your focus should not be on winning as many points as possible; it should be on gaining your main objective.

The Deal-Killing Bonus

A dealmaker, or negotiator, is really just a good salesman, so he should try to heed all the prudent rules that apply to good salesmanship. And every good salesman knows the danger of kicking an open door; i.e., continuing to sell after the prospect has already agreed to buy.

The smart salesman or negotiator knows when to stop selling and negotiating and develops the self-discipline to act accordingly. The more you talk, the more you increase your chances of saying something that may open a can of worms and kill a deal at the eleventh hour. In particular, never get carried away and introduce into a deal one or more after-the-fact bonuses in the form of new ideas, people, or thoughts. This can prove to be a very costly mistake, one that often results in reopening negotiations, or, worse, killing a deal that was already in the bag.

Such impulsive action calls to mind a deal I had been negotiating for a couple of months when I was quite inexperienced. It involved an investor from Philadelphia regarding a distributorship for a high-quality line of health-care products. I had already made two trips to Philadelphia to discuss the deal with him, and we had spoken by phone about a dozen times. During each meeting and telephone discussion, we edged ever closer to agreeing to the terms of a deal, until finally, after my second trip to Philadelphia, we ironed out the final details, shook hands on a verbal agreement, and I flew back to the West Coast.

We then spoke again by phone and set up a closing date in Philadelphia. Having been involved in more than one deal in the past where the other party failed to do what he said he was going to do, I took the trouble, during our telephone discussion, to carefully review each point we had agreed upon. I wanted to be certain that there was no miscommunication between us before making the long trip back to Philadelphia. The investor was the impatient type, and several times during my review he interrupted me with comments like, "Hey, relax, it's a done deal." I guess it's something in my genetic makeup, but the more times he repeated the words *done deal*, the more uncomfortable I became.

Politely brushing aside his assurances, I persisted in my review of the points. The last item I brought up was something called *money*. It hadn't gone unnoticed by me over the years that the words "write a check" seem to do funny things to people—like make them frown, or quiver, or transform into Darth Vader, or do something more subtle, like threaten me with a hunting knife. So I clearly and slowly said to him, "And then, *you'll write me a check for $200,000.*"

The investor impatiently replied, "Yes, yes. I said we've got a deal. Just fly to Philadelphia and let's get this thing closed."

And that's when I did something that forever qualified me for the **All-World Entrepreneurial Dumb Team**. Even though we supposedly had a deal, my insecurity led me to throw in an afterthought bonus just to put the icing on the cake. Displaying an alarming lack of self-discipline, I blurted out, "I have a great idea. Why don't I invite a couple of the top marketing people from this company to come to Philadelphia and meet with us? Then we can talk about the company's future plans just before or after the closing, and kill two birds with one stone." The investor liked my idea and told me to go ahead and set everything up.

After flying to Philadelphia, the investor and I met with Legalman and reviewed the final details of the closing. Then, after finishing our review, Legalman went to his office to dictate the final changes to his secretary, assuring us that the papers would be ready for signing in an hour or so. To pass the time, the investor and I made small talk, waiting until either Legalman brought in the closing documents or the marketing people showed up. For the sake of making conversation, I again casually started to review some of the points of the deal, and again the investor interrupted me, sighed, and said, "Boy, you really are the nervous type. It's a done deal, forget it. Let's just concentrate on the game plan for marketing these products."

Just about that time, the marketing people arrived, and we decided to meet with them right away since the final draft of the agreement was not yet completed. Unless you, too, are a member of the **All-World Entrepreneurial Dumb Team**, you probably wouldn't believe what took place at that meeting. For a battle-scarred entrepreneur like me, it was like living through *The Texas Chainsaw Massacre*. Every time one of the marketing executives spoke, the investor would say something like, "Hmm, I didn't know that. Why is that so?" Or, "You mean you can't really be sure of that? Then it might require more money than we'll have available?" With each passing moment, it got worse . . . and worse . . . and worse.

I, of course, took it very well, crying out loud only twice and using up only one box of Kleenex. After the meeting, the investor and I went to what was supposed to have been the closing room, and waited for Legalman to bring in the closing documents. But there was an inexplicable feeling in the air that made me uncomfortable, so I casually started reviewing some of the closing points again. As quickly as possible, I got to the words that must be spoken, sooner or later, at every closing—what I like to refer to as the "getting paid" words—virtually the same words I had uttered to the investor on the phone before committing to come to Philadelphia: "And *then*, you'll give *me* the check for $200,000 . . ."

Whereupon the investor interrupted me with—you guessed it—"What check?" And people wonder why our mental institutions are overflowing with psychotic entrepreneurs foaming at the mouth?

The investor then went into a long dissertation, saying that he apologized profusely if there had been a "miscommunication," but that he had no idea I was coming in from the West Coast with the intention of closing a deal. He insisted he had been under the impression that the purpose of our meeting was to talk to the marketing people, after which we would see if we could agree on a marketing plan (whatever that was supposed to mean). Then, so went his story, we were supposed to decide whether we could work out a deal, and, if so, set up a closing.

Quite an interesting miscommunication, given the fact that nothing remotely close to any of this had ever been discussed by either of us previously, and the marketing people were there only as a result of a stupid afterthought on my part. Further, not one word about any of this had been mentioned when the investor, Legalman, and I had reviewed the final closing points just prior to the marketing people showing up, nor when Legalman said he was going to dictate the final corrections for the closing documents.

I had to confess to myself that, through an inexcusable lack of self-discipline, it was I alone who had been responsible for reopening a done deal. I had thoughtlessly and impulsively introduced new people into the deal before it was officially closed . . . and, as a result, ended up taking a rickshaw back to the West Coast.

Lifetime Membership

Since I seem to be on a dumb roll here, I might as well let you hear The Big Dumb—how I one-upped myself, outdoing even my Philadelphia caper. This is the one that put me on the **All-Time, All-World Entrepreneurial Dumb Team**, the classic act-on-impulse-and-live-to-regret-it mistake.

Long before I had written my first book, I was involved in a corporation with a wealthy partner who had a tidy little financial statement of about $13 million (a figure closer to $40 million in today's dollars). After a long series of negotiations, our corporation agreed to buy a printing plant for a substantial amount of cash and a promissory note of approximately $500,000. Everything was a go, except the owners of the printing plant wanted my wealthy partner to personally guarantee the note. He finally agreed to do so, and at that point the deal was seemingly done.

However, at the closing, one of the two sellers blurted out, kind of as an afterthought, "Why don't you (yes, *me*) guarantee the note, too?" To which I chuckled in return, "If Frank can't pay the $500,000, it sure isn't going to do you any good to have me on the note. He's worth $13 million; I'm worth $11.83 (which was an exaggeration, since I had forgotten to deduct the $5.50 service charge from my last bank statement). The seller, with an I-may-as-well-give-it-one-more-try attitude, retorted, "If that's true, then what's the difference? If you're not worth anything, and Frank has the big financial statement, what have you got to lose? It just shows some added good faith on your part."

The seller was not noted for having oversized brain cells, so I think he just got lucky, but, in point of fact, he had said exactly what someone in his position should say. The rule is, whenever you have everything to gain and nothing to lose, ask. One never knows what strange turns life may take down the road. On the other hand, my severe case of impulsivitis was not yet in remission, so I said exactly what someone in my position should *not* say: "Okay, no big deal. It's meaningless, but I'll do it."

Years later, here are the strange turns that life had taken:

(1) Long after I had disassociated myself from the company that had bought the printing plant, it was not able to pay the note.

(2) My ex-partner, after a record-setting string of masochistic financial decisions, filed for bankruptcy.

(3) And; in the interim, guess who became a highly visible, bestselling author with a bank balance considerably higher than $11.83? A bank balance, I should add, that soon was reduced by an amount of about $500,000.

To this day, I'm certain that had I held my ground and refused to guarantee the note, the seller would have shrugged it off and the deal still would have closed. It was an expensive way to learn that when the urge to say *yes* comes over you in situations where the down side has the potential to be catastrophic, that's precisely when you need the self-discipline to say *no*. To my chagrin, I learned the hard way that an impulsive *yes* can have devastating consequences for years to come. In the most extreme cases, it can permanently damage a person's life.

The Lazy Man's Way to Disaster

One of the most costly results of an individual's failure to embrace the Self-Discipline Habit is that he continually falls victim to the dreaded Assumption Trap. The words *I assumed* comprise one of the most dangerous phrases in the English language. Everyone past the Age of Infinite Wisdom is all too aware that it's unwise to assume anything, yet most people stumble through life over a road laced with land-mine assumptions.

An important step toward avoiding the Assumption Trap is to learn to translate Assumptionese. For example, "I assume" usually means, "I'm just too lazy to check out the facts." "No problem" in Assumptionese means, "I told someone else to take care of it, so it's not *my* problem." And so it goes. Most people will expend incredible amounts of energy to avoid expending the energy needed to do the job they were asked to do in the first place.

It's an amazing phenomenon, but there seems to be a totally unwarranted, broadly accepted assumption on the part of the public that someone, somewhere, is in control of everything. However, the longer I live, the more convinced I am that *no one* is in control of *anything*. The fact is that we're living on a runaway planet! There's only one safe assumption in life: The person who assures you that everything is all right is all wrong.

"Being There"

I've given the Assumption Trap a lot of thought since seeing an intriguing movie several years ago. The movie, *Being There*, starred the late Peter Sellers. It's about a functionally illiterate gardener, played by Sellers, who had never been outside of his own yard until well into middle age. Suddenly, through a series of bizarre happenstances, he is brought into Washington's inner circles and hailed as a brilliant statesman.

Because the illiterate gardener has had almost no experience in communicating, when he is asked his name, he mutters his occupation instead: gardener. As a result, the political power brokers mistakenly conclude that his name is Chauncey Gardener. He is interviewed on television, invited to the White House to meet the president, and introduced to the city's elite at a series of gala affairs. As the movie concludes, political insiders are considering the possibility of having Chauncey run for president because of his "impeccable qualifications."

While it would appear that *Being There* is nothing more than a farfetched comedy about incompetence rising to the top, I have my own theory about the film's success. Deep down within the recesses of even the most ignorant and naive moviegoer's brain is the uncomfortable feeling that *Being There* depicts real life. Consider:

- The people who rule the country—congressmen, the presidents, the Supreme Court justices, and the bureaucrats. How would you explain to an alien from another planet how the worst among us—people who are truly malevolent, ignorant, or both—managed to get elected or appointed to positions of great power?

- I once had a business relationship with a well-known "psychotherapist" who, to this day, frequently appears on national television (always introduced as a psychologist) and offers advice to millions of viewers, yet doesn't even have a degree in psychology! Further, I've been present on numerous occasions when this "psychologist" has, behind closed doors, screamed and yelled hysterically, cried uncontrollably, or both.

  Off camera, he uses foul language in virtually every sentence and admits to never reading newspapers, magazines, or books. Early on, I was surprised to find that it was difficult for a reasonably well informed person to even discuss psychology with him, because he simply hadn't read much about the subject. Nevertheless, this *Being There* individual is still billed as an expert psychologist on television, and millions of people assume that he is eminently qualified. After all, if he weren't, why would he be on television?

- Another *Being There* example that comes to mind was passed along to me by a brilliant heart specialist who once told me that a certain nationally renowned heart surgeon was a bona-fide joke among medical students at the university where he taught. While being given national attention for supposedly miraculous achievements in heart surgery, the consensus among his peers was that he shouldn't be performing surgery at all due to his age and lack of surgical skills.

I'm sure you could cite similar *Being There* examples from your own experience. The question is, how do such people manage to get into positions of wealth, fame, and/or power? How are they able to delude the public into believing they are something other than what they really are?

In many cases, it's because we generally assume that what we hear on television and read in print or on the Internet represents truth. Unfortunately, a large percentage of the time, nothing could be *further* from the truth. Therefore, you have to exercise the self-discipline to work at seeing what is, rather than what seems to be. Again, Buddha gave us sound advice when he said, "Believe nothing, no matter where you read it, or who said it, no matter if I have said it, unless it agrees with your own reason and your own common sense."

The Long Way to Toronto
One of the most time-wasting experiences of my life occurred in the early 1970s, and was a direct result of my falling into the Assumption Trap. In Chapter 5, I mentioned that a business associate and I had purchased a controlling interest in an American Stock Exchange company. My associate, John, was perhaps the most action-oriented individual I've ever known, but, as is often the case with action types, he was totally unconcerned with details. His complete disregard for facts and planning often created an amazing entanglement of problems, situations so bizarre they could have passed for slapstick-comedy skits.

To close the deal, we needed to borrow $1.8 million. John had a long-standing relationship with the chief operating officer of a bank in London, going back to the days when the banker (who was an American) had lived in the United States. However, John had not dealt with him since the banker had moved to England. John told me that if I would agree to go to London and talk to the banker about the loan, he would call ahead of time and set everything up.

I was delighted to have the opportunity to walk into a roll-out-the-carpet situation, and as soon as John spoke with his banker friend, I booked my flight to London. It was an exhausting, all-night trip, and when I arrived in London about 9 a.m., I hopped in a cab and went directly to the bank. I introduced myself to the receptionist and was soon led into the banker's office. Exhaustion aside, I was totally focused on the $1.8 million loan I hoped to obtain.

The banker and I exchanged pleasantries, after which he got right to the point and asked, "Well, Mr. Ringer, what can I do for you?" I explained that my partner and I wanted to borrow $1.8 million to buy control of an American Stock Exchange company, whereupon he interrupted me and said, "Oh, I'm afraid you've come to the wrong branch. That would be considered a venture-capital loan, and we only make conventional loans here. You'll have to see the people at our Toronto branch."

As I walked out the front door of the bank, I thought to myself, "I must make it a point to fly to London more often. What a perfectly delightful experience." There's nothing quite as exhilarating as flying across the ocean, staggering half asleep into a bank, meeting with the chief loan officer for five minutes, and being told that you've come to the wrong branch and that the branch you have to see is an hour's flying time from where you started. But at least I was assured of a continuing spot on the **All-Time, All-World Entrepreneurial Dumb Team**.

When I reached Heathrow Airport, I called John in the States and put on an Oscar-winning performance of pretending as though it was no big deal. "John," I queried, "I thought you said you had already discussed this matter with your banker? He had no idea what I had come to talk to him about, and right off the bat told me that I'd have to talk to the bank's Toronto branch about this kind of loan."

"Well, of course I didn't go into detail with him over the phone," snapped John. "I just told him I would appreciate it if he would meet with an associate of mine about a deal we were working on together. No sense trying to explain the deal long distance."

I stopped chewing the phone cord just long enough to smile and say, "I fully understand, John. I just assumed you had already explained the deal to him. What do you suggest now?"

Without a pause, John said, "Look, I'll call the Toronto branch and explain the whole thing to them, then you can fly straight to Toronto. Call me back in a half hour."

Sure enough, when I called back, John had spoken to the Toronto branch and set up another appointment for—would you believe?—later that day! "No problem," I assured him, "I'll be there." I wrote down all the pertinent information—names, telephone numbers, and addresses—and, after bidding John farewell, called the bank's branch in Toronto and asked to speak with the officer with whom I was to meet. I not only reconfirmed our appointment, but also explained the deal to him in detail. I was not about to assume anything. Then, *after* he had assured me that his bank would be interested, I departed for Toronto.

Luckily, the story had a happy ending, because the loan eventually was granted. However, unless you want to end up in bizarre situations like flying to England for a five-minute rejection, don't assume that someone else has checked the facts. If it's your body that's going to take the punishment, it's up to you to have the self-discipline to do the checking before swinging into action. The bigger the stakes, the more true this is, especially when you approach pay dirt. **Real-World Rule No. 357: At the moment of truth, never risk a fumble. When the ball is on the one-yard line, carry it over yourself.**

The Reality of Miscommunications

Speaking of costly assumptions, it's also important to remember **Real-World Rule No. 244: The degree of miscommunication regarding what's been agreed upon in a business deal tends to increase in direct proportion to the amount of money involved.**

Never assume that all parties to an important meeting have the same understanding of what's been agreed upon. I make it a practice to take copious notes at all such meetings, then have the notes copied and ask that everyone present review them before leaving. I also read the notes aloud, then ask if anyone has any questions. If someone misunderstands, or disagrees, with one of the points, we talk it out, make the appropriate corrections, again have the notes copied, and repeat the same process until everyone agrees on what has been agreed upon.

Does this totally eliminate misunderstandings? No, of course not. Life isn't that simple. However, if one of the parties decides he wants to change, or back out of, the deal, it does make it much more difficult for him to use the phony excuse that "apparently there was a miscommunication between us."

The Fascinating Tale of Ms. Best

Interviewing prospective employees is another area where I've learned the hard way to adhere to the Self-Discipline Habit when it comes to making assumptions. In an age when young people believe they should be rewarded for just being alive, a large percentage of job applicants have a remarkably inflated perception of their abilities.

Many applicants today can't even spell the word *competency*, let alone display it in their work. Therefore, it's a dangerous mistake to assume that just because someone talks confidently in an interview, he is what he appears to be. There's many a slip between the interview and a person's performance on the job.

My own frustrating experience in this area has taught me to be especially wary when an individual makes too forceful a case for himself. It seems as though a whole cult of people has grown up who, lacking skill, competence, and/or ambition, have become amazingly adept at fooling interviewers. The objective today isn't to become competent at a job; it's to become competent at being interviewed. Early in my career, I thought I was quite good at judging prospects during interviews, but, without being consciously aware of it, I apparently lost pace with the rapid proliferation of interviewee tricks.

My memory takes me back to a frantic search for a high-level "executive secretary." (I use quote marks around the words *executive secretary*, because it seems as though anyone who knows how to type fifty words a minute, talks in an authoritative tone on the telephone, and has managed to stay with one employer for at least six months fancies himself an executive secretary.)

After interviewing a number of prospects, one candidate in particular made a big impression on me with her air of self-confidence. In fact, at one point she just came right out and told me, in a matter-of-fact tone, that she was "the best." Of course, because she was the best, she also wanted a starting salary that was far in excess of anything I had previously paid to anyone who was an unproven talent. You're probably thinking, "Well, knowing Ringer, he took the bait." And you're right.

Naively, I assumed this young lady must, at least, be very good. Otherwise, how would she have the nerve to come right out and say she was the best? To make such a bold statement, she must have *something* to back it up with, I reasoned. Since I was not able to contact her previous employer (naturally, he was out of business, apparently living in Singapore or somewhere, and unavailable for comment), I based my hiring of her on assumptions.

The result? After a couple of weeks, I noticed a few things that Ms. Best was doing wrong, but I wasn't too concerned about them, because I had the comfort of knowing that she was "the best."

After all, she had told me so. While tactfully complimenting her on her "progress," I also casually suggested that there were a few areas where she might want to sharpen up a bit—such as trying not to make so many assumptions herself (which seemed to be leading her to make numerous mistakes), being more alert when listening to dictation (so as to make fewer of those mistakes), and cutting down on her social calls during business hours (always a mistake).

By the third month, I was ready to concede that Ms. Best was not "the best" after all. To those in the office who were thinking more in terms of setting the back of her hair on fire, I said, "Look, maybe she isn't the superstar I thought she was, but she is good. She just seems to have mental lapses now and then."

By the end of the fourth month, I was beginning to weaken. "All right, I admit she makes a lot of mistakes. I admit she sometimes forgets to write down phone messages. I admit she has a habit of making costly assumptions. But she *is* mechanically proficient," I protested to my troops in desperation.

By the fifth month, it was I who was considering putting a torch to her hair. I finally threw in the towel one day when I called Ms. Best into my office to point out another mistake she had made, one which had resulted in some costly repercussions. My primary intent was to forestall a repetition of the unhappy event, but she didn't let it go at that. Her first reaction was to tell me it was I who was mistaken, because my recollection of my instructions to her was incorrect. After I strongly suggested that my instructions had been as I had stated, Ms. Best broke into tears and ran out of my office. It certainly was a touching sight— extraordinarily appropriate business behavior for an "executive secretary."

Subsequently, she reviewed her transcription notes and found, to her chagrin, that she had been wrong. Did that prompt her to offer a brief and immediate apology? Of course not. That's not the way "the best" operate. Instead, she typed up a two-page explanation of the situation—on company time—in which she admitted her mistake, but emphasized that "(my) handling of the situation begged for defensive action on (her) part."

At that point, I realized that I had an important decision to make: Either I had to go into the professional baby-sitting business full time or admit to the rest of the office that I had been guilty of making an embarrassing and incorrect assumption. I decided on the latter. Not only was Ms. Best guilty of all the aforementioned mistakes, but, my previous assertions notwithstanding, she really was not even mechanically proficient.

Alas, the truth had to be acknowledged. If Ms. Best was "the best," I was the Dalai Lama. She was not the best; she was not good; she was not average; she was not even bad. She was, in point of fact, the *worst* secretary I had ever hired—a living, breathing, full-fledged incompetent, fit only for employment by a government agency.

Job applicants with inflated self-perceptions are primarily guilty of self-delusion; i.e., they base their actions on who and what they would like to be, rather than who and what they are. Get in the habit of not assuming that someone is even marginally competent, let alone great, no matter how good he claims to be. Instead, have the self-discipline to make him prove it. And if he's not willing to prove it, have the self-discipline to say: "Thanks, but I pass."

Winning by Default

David Seabury succinctly expressed a great deal of wisdom when he stated, "The hero is not impulsive. He prepares." One of the best aids to bolster your self-discipline is to make it a point to be prepared.

Basically, preparation involves two areas. First is factual and/ or tangible preparation, which includes figures, documents, and various materials that can aid you in stating your case in a favorable manner. Second is psychological preparation, the ultimate of which is to mentally rehearse a variety of likely scenarios in advance. By anticipating an objection before a meeting takes place, you're in a position to head it off in the event someone brings it up. Better still, you yourself can raise the question of a potential obstacle before the other side even thinks of it, phrasing it in such a way that it appears to be an item that can be handled with ease.

Having just related a couple of zingers about myself, it may seem hard to believe, but one of my greatest strengths is having the self-discipline to prepare. My numerous past indiscretions in this area have caused me to become fanatically disciplined when it comes to preparation. "If I had eight hours to chop down a tree, I'd spend six sharpening my axe," said Abraham Lincoln. I'd like to tell you that Abe stole that line from me, but you'd never buy it.

Nonetheless, I normally practice this philosophy when I undertake a project. I like to lay the groundwork slowly and carefully, then, when all is in place, sprint to the finish line. Before I meet with someone to make a presentation or discuss a business proposal, I make certain that I do my homework. It's wise to go into a meeting armed with the facts. In the words of Pythagoras, "Numbers have a way of taking a man by the hand and leading him down the path of reason."

Since most people rarely are well prepared, I look at it almost like winning by default. If you and I are otherwise even in all pertinent aspects of a deal, you lose. Why? Because unless I fall into one of my rare laziness lapses, I will outprepare you. My objective, quite frankly, is to literally overwhelm you with preparation. I'm not one of those people who enjoys close games; I like victories that are as one-sided as a plane crash.

This isn't arrogance on my part. On the contrary, I freely admit that it takes no innate skill or intelligence. I learned to do it, because I observed, through firsthand experience, that it leads to big payoffs. And the more big payoffs I achieved, the more motivated I became to be prepared. On reflection, many of my greatest successes have been a result of superior preparation, while many of my worst failures can be traced to a lack of preparation. This is an area where I've personally experienced just how fine the line between stupendous success and colossal failure can be.

Two of the most important reasons for being prepared are that (1) circumstances continually change, and (2) the chances of a deal closing are inversely proportional to the amount of time that elapses between a verbal agreement and a closing. In other words, being prepared puts you in a position to get the deal closed as quickly as possible.

A Rare Defeat for Legalman

One of the big payoffs I was alluding to came in the late Sixties when I spent many months negotiating the purchase of a company from an indecisive principal. Every time I thought the deal was set, Legalman would come up with one reason or another why his client shouldn't, or couldn't, go through with the deal. Legalman, of course, was well aware that he would no longer be in a position to siphon off legal fees from the company's coffers once the deal closed, so, of course, it was obvious that he intended to fight the sale to the bitter end. Absolutely no scheme or ploy was beneath him; shame or embarrassment was not even an issue.

Unfortunately for Legalman, due to my impeccable preparation I was always one step ahead of him, so, notwithstanding his treachery, we kept inching ever closer to a closing. Finally, all documentation was in order and the deal was set to close at—of all places—the Pierre Hotel in New York. Because I so respected Legalman's tenacity and resourcefulness for coming up with ever more absurd reasons why his client shouldn't go through with the sale, I went overboard to prepare for this particular closing.

I played through a hundred different scenarios and reasons that Legalman might be inclined to use in an attempt to block the closing, or, at least, have it postponed. I had documentation piled to the ceiling, paper clips properly poised, and staplers ready to be thrust into action on a moment's notice. I was *ready*.

The reviewing of documents and stalling went on throughout the afternoon, until Legalman finally was able to get a stay of execution by insisting we break for dinner. Checkmate: I was successful in convincing everyone that we should have dinner in the suite and keep right on reviewing documents.

As the hours rolled by, I sensed that Legalman was getting to his client in subtle ways, and, sure enough, around 12:30 a.m., just after Legalman whispered something in his client's ear, the client got up and nervously announced, "I'm sorry, but I just can't go through with this deal." Whereupon he and his two top aides departed with Legalman. "End of deal," I thought to myself. "What a great story this would make for a book." (Who knew?)

After a philosophical discourse with *my* Legalman, I was just about ready to call it a night and write it off as just one of those things, when the doorbell rang. Startled, I looked at my watch and saw that it was 1:30 a.m. I opened the door, and there, to my surprise, stood the seller and his entourage, including a very miffed-looking Legalman. The seller said, "You know, we just walked around the block a few times, and I thought to myself, 'What am I afraid of, anyway?' I decided to act on my gut instincts and go through with the deal. Let's get on with the signing of the papers."

It's surprise moments like this when being prepared really pays off. Had Legalman been given enough time, I think he might have managed to swing the pendulum of doubt back in the other direction once again, which probably would have been ended the deal once and for all. But once I got the go-ahead, I was in a position to move swiftly. Not only was every document in perfect order, they were already opened to the required signature pages. Within minutes, all documents were signed, sealed, and delivered, and, just like that, the deal that had been off an hour earlier was now done.

While it's true that life can be unfair, and you cannot prevent the inevitable, it's also true that when the breaks do come your way, as they did for me on that memorable night at the Pierre Hotel, you have to be prepared and ready to take advantage of them. Remember, breaks float in and out of people's lives every day without being exploited.

Your Greatest Ally

When I talk about being prepared in order to take advantage of the breaks, it's back to relying on the law of averages. If you believe in the law of averages—and, hopefully, by now that isn't even an issue—you know it's just a matter of time until you get your share of breaks. Time goes hand-in-hand with being prepared, and time is where your self-discipline is really put to the test. Time will always come to your rescue, provided you have the self-discipline to stay prepared. Patience isn't a virtue when it comes to getting results; it's a necessity. Once again, it's hard to improve on the words of Baltasar Gracian, who declared so simply, yet so profoundly, "Time and I against any other two."

The late Chinn Ho, the fabulously wealthy Hawaiian who was frequently referred to as the Chinese Rockefeller, once said in an interview that one secret of his great financial success was that he practiced the philosophy, "Wait long, then move fast." In other words, he had the self-discipline to wait for the right opportunity, then, when it arrived, he moved swiftly to take advantage of it.

Perhaps the epitome of demonstrating the Self-Discipline Habit when it came to the philosophy of waiting long, then moving fast, was demonstrated by the legendary Boston Red Sox slugger, Ted Williams. In the view of many, Williams was the greatest hitter of all time. In an article about Williams many years ago, he was quoted as saying that in the course of a game, he expected to see only one perfect pitch. Considering that a batter usually receives anywhere from twenty to fifty pitches per game, I found Williams's statement to be fascinating. He said that because he had no idea when that one perfect pitch would appear, he knew it was crucial to have the self-discipline to be both patient and prepared.

As a business philosophy, Williams' strategy is invaluable. Experience has convinced me that it never fails to pay big dividends over the long term.

Part-time Versus Full-time Self-Discipline

Being a self-disciplined person is what the Self-Discipline Habit is all about. Just to be clear, there's a big difference between being self-disciplined in a certain situation at a certain time and being a consistently self-disciplined person. Anyone can display self-discipline on occasion, but to achieve consistently positive results takes consistency. It's the day-in, day-out practice of self-discipline that determines where you'll be at the end of a week, a month, a year, or a lifetime. Remember, a lifetime is nothing more than an accumulation of years, months, weeks, and days, and what takes place in those smaller increments of time will determine whether or not your life, on the whole, is successful.

If you aspire to play with the heavy hitters, you can't coast. You have to be prepared to play every point as though it were match point. In other words, you have to be consistently focused. Dabblers are rarely, if ever, successful. It's when you focus totally, intensely, and consistently on one project—a project that has the potential to yield a worthwhile payoff—that you have the greatest chance for success.

You must have the self-discipline not to allow others to pull you off course with side projects or unrelated ventures. You must have the self-discipline to keep your mind from wandering toward thoughts of what else you should be doing, who slighted you last week, how you're going to clear up some bothersome financial problem, and a thousand-and-one other concerns that perpetually and randomly bombard your mind. You must make it a habit to block out those things that do not contribute to the creative process.

Anyone who has ever written a book knows that it controlled attention is critical to success. The most difficult project in the world is to start from a blank document on your computer every day, then have the self-discipline to stay with it for hours at a time without interruption.

This is true of any profession, not just writing. Your success in getting results is directly tied to the number of hours you consistently devote to quiet, intense, uninterrupted, creative thinking. If you discipline yourself to do this four to six hours a day, you'll be astonished by the results. To paraphrase the turn-of-the-century advertising legend Claude Hopkins, what appears to be genius is often nothing more than "the art of taking pains."

The Exception
Talk about inhabiting a world of delusions, the word *exception* itself is delusive, because in the real world exceptions are rarely the nonrecurring phenomena people would like to believe they are. In fact, the Self-Discipline Habit and The Exception are at opposite ends of the success spectrum.

Because it so graphically illustrates my point about The Exception, I'd like to use another nonbusiness example from my personal experience, one which again is equally applicable to the business world. Years ago, I found out the hard way about the delusive nature of The Exception when I began rationalizing about my eating habits. It seemed as if every day I was saying to myself, "Well, I've already blown it today, so I may as well enjoy myself." My rationalizations in this area came to an end after an episode I nostalgically refer to as The Battle of Little Big Pie.

Many years earlier, I had pared more than fifty pounds off my Christie-like body. Since that time, I had taken great care to watch my caloric intake and adhere to a vigorous exercise program. Then, one day, I allowed myself to make an exception—which was followed by another exception . . . which was followed by another . . . and another . . . and another. Just about the time my weight was beginning to get out of hand, I happened to go to Palm Springs for a quiet weekend. By that time, I had renewed my old habit of nibbling. I nibbled everything in sight—candy, potato chips, tree bark, index cards—anything that fell into my path.

As I waddled down the streets of Palm Springs, looking like *The Thing*, people screamed as I approached. However, I hadn't even scratched the surface of my caloric potential. My true, championship form didn't show itself until Saturday evening when I was having dinner with an old friend from the East Coast. As I sat in that Palm Springs restaurant, panting and perspiring as I ate, my friend tactfully mentioned that it looked as if I had "put on a little weight." (I suspected his remark was prompted by the fact I had eaten all the bread on the table and had started to butter my left forefinger.)

Finally, I came right out with it: "I don't know how this got started, but lately I've been eating like a wild boar. Now I've already gone so far over the line that nothing else I eat tonight could make much difference. It's already a lost weekend, so I may as well go all the way."

That was the go-ahead signal to totally desert my self-discipline. You could hear the theme music to *Rocky* playing in the background as I mounted a ground offensive against the kitchen. My friend and his wife trembled in awe, expressing fear, then disbelief, when at last I ordered dessert. The piece of coconut cream pie that the waiter brought me must have been the largest portion ever served to a mammal west of the Rockies. I got the distinct feeling the waiter was mocking me.

I remember my friend asking me, incredulously, "Are you going to eat that whole thing?" I was already disgusted with myself, so why not go for it? What difference would another few thousand calories make? I must immodestly tell you that it was an incredible finish, right out of the movie *Fatso*. Everyone in the restaurant who had thrilled to Dom De Luise and his pals chanting, in unison, "Get the honey," couldn't help but feel a twinge of excitement as my head fell forward into my plate. I had done it. I had gone the distance with that gargantuan piece of pie.

I awoke the next morning with a pounding foodover, and realized that it was either a return to no exceptions or back to the way things had been years before when my life had been devoid of self-discipline. The decision wasn't hard to make. One glance at an old picture of myself was all it took. In that worn-out, crumpled photo, I looked like an experiment gone wrong—a corpulent cross between Wimpy and Michael Moore. I mean to tell you, I was big. They say no man is an island, but I came close. And why not? In the old days, I had set world records in the freestyle banana split competition and the wind-aided buttered-popcorn dash. The way I ate, I was lucky the universe was expanding.

After the Palm Springs eatfest, I caught hold of myself and admitted that my exceptions had again become the rule. Eating out of disgust was once more becoming a way of life. I got just close enough to my old self to get a glimpse of what the long-term consequences would be if I didn't staple my lips together. Beginning the next day, it was back to a delightful life of consistency, no exceptions, and liking myself again. Best of all, I escaped my old niche of being a perennial contender for the Fatty Arbuckle Award, and began having delusions of grandeur when I looked in the mirror. "Eat your heart out, Arnold," I thought to myself as I flexed my awesome three-inch biceps.

Putting the Fun Back in Life

Through the process of association, the experience I just related to you has paid big dividends in helping me avoid exceptions in my business life, particularly when it comes to creative projects. I now find little difficulty concentrating for hours at a time without a break.

The problem with The Exception can be summed up best by **Real-World Rule No. 28: Every exception a person makes brings him closer to a life where the exception becomes the rule, until life becomes one big exception.** About all you can say about such an individual is that he leads a very exceptional life.

Isn't it true that there's always a special game, a special event, or a special circumstance to tempt you? And isn't there always someone around to chide you, "Aw, c'mon, just this one time. What's the big deal? It's not going to kill you." Maybe it won't kill you, but little by little exceptions will destroy your life. So it's at those moments when you're being most pressured to make exceptions that you find out just how strong your self-discipline is. The question is, is it strong enough for you to look the other person in the eye and say, "No!" without hesitation?

I realize some people might argue that being self-disciplined to the point of trying to eliminate all exceptions leads to a grim existence. However, I've found just the opposite to be true. I feel the more you like to play, the more self-disciplined you should be. Why? Because if you understand that there's no such thing as something for nothing, you'll be anxious to pay now so you can play later—without the Guilt Fairy looking over your shoulder and watching your every move.

It's not a matter of being perfect; rather, it's a matter of *striving* for perfection. Just because you can never be perfect doesn't mean you shouldn't strive to do your best. Which means that when you do weaken—when you make an exception—you should try not to delude yourself about it. Instead, acknowledge that it happened and cut your losses before they get out of hand. Catch yourself before you go from bad to worse; one more exception *does* hurt.

Just because you had a bad morning at the office doesn't mean you should squander the rest of the day. Anyone can do well on good days, but only truly successful people—those who adhere to the Self-Discipline Habit—consistently make headway on bad days. No matter how many exceptions you've already made on a bad day, making one more isn't going to make matters better. It will only make them worse. Develop the habit of turning bad days, bad weeks, and bad months around by having the self-discipline to stop yourself before things get out of hand.

The Self-Discipline Habit leads positive results, and positive results lead to a more enjoyable life. And, remember, to be a self-disciplined person, as opposed to being *occasionally* self-disciplined, you can't coast; you've got to do it every day.

CHAPTER 10

THE ACTION HABIT

Theodore Roosevelt once confessed, "There is nothing brilliant nor outstanding in my record, except perhaps this one thing: I do the things that I believe ought to be done . . . And when I make up my mind to do a thing, I act."

Without the Action Habit, the other nine major success habits I've covered in this book aren't of much use. Until action is taken, they are little more than theory, because results are not possible without action. Theories are nice, but ultimately they have to implemented. The very state of being alive implies action.

In Chapter 1, I pointed out that one of the basic realities of life is that knowledge without wisdom is useless. An even more frustrating reality of life is that even if you possess knowledge *and* wisdom, the two of them together still are useless without action. This is the other side of the self-discipline coin in regard to being prepared. Everything in life works better in moderation, and too much preparation can become an excuse for indefinitely postponing action. In other words, you have to avoid falling in love with planning and strategizing to an extreme that it becomes an end in itself. No matter how much planning you do, it's impossible to project solutions to most day-to-day problems.

I had a friend who was absolutely enamored with working on projections for a great idea he had for a service business.

He worked away on his computer for two years, and while circumstances continued to change regarding the industry he was planning to enter, he kept right on revising his projections. One day I visited him and was puzzled by the excitement he displayed. He had just revised his figures again, and said, "Can you believe what these computer programs can do? Watch this: If I change just one figure on my projected cash-flow chart, all the other figures change instantaneously. Isn't that unbelievable?"

To which I responded, "Yes, it's great—but you're going broke."

My friend had allowed himself to get sidetracked by something I discussed earlier—confusing the means with the end. He had become so carried away with his computer's capacity, not to mention his own computer skills, that he had forgotten his original objective. It was not to become an expert at doing cash-flow projections; it was to find a way to convert his idea into a profitable enterprise. Planning is a vital, first step to getting results, but it can never be a substitute for action. You can never reach second base if you don't take your foot off first base.

You've often heard the expression that "ideas are a dime a dozen." Yet, an idea can change the world—and many have. All that is meant by the dime-a-dozen cliché is that an idea, of an by itself, has no intrinsic value. It must be accompanied by action. In this respect, an idea really is the first step in the success chain, with preparation and planning comprising the second, and action the third.

I like to half jokingly tell audiences that I "invented" Federal Express. And it's true. However, I'm sure that thousands of other entrepreneurs and wannabe entrepreneurs also did. When I was attempting to put deals together all over the country during the late Sixties, continually fighting deadlines and trying to get documents to distant cities as quickly as possible, it occurred to me that it would be a great service business to offer overnight delivery of important papers to people like myself. In fact, I thought about it off and on for years . . . while someone named Fred Smith came along and actually did it.

The moral is to be found in an old adage that says: The successful implementation of one good idea is worth more than a thousand good ideas not acted upon.

Who wants to invent Fed Ex? I'd much rather own it.

Roadblocks to Making Things Happen

To develop the Action Habit, you have to overcome the mental obstacles that prevent people from taking action. I've already discussed the most fundamental reason of all for failing to take action: lack of meaning in one's life. Whenever you feel inertia (the disinclination to act) overtaking you, you should go back to the five Present Living Questions discussed in Chapter 4.

The last suggestion I made in that chapter was to step back and review your progress periodically, and if you don't seem to be getting where you want to be in life, reevaluate your answers. If you haven't answered the Present Living Questions honestly, or if circumstances have changed in such a way as to make your original answers invalid, it's easy to slip into a state of inertia and feel as if there's no reason to get up in the morning. But if you feel confident that your answers are still valid—which should take the form of a strong inner desire to achieve one or more objectives— yet something seems to be preventing you from taking action, the answer probably lies in searching for other obstacles that may be stifling you, then finding ways to deal with them.

In analyzing my own periods of inaction over the years, I've come up with six major roadblocks to making things happen, all of which are primarily mental in nature. That's an exciting realization, because it means that freeing yourself from an action-jam is primarily a mental problem, and mental problems can always be resolved.

In other words, once the mental obstacle is removed, action follows almost automatically. Even more exciting about this is the fact that, as with the other major success habits discussed in this book, the Action Habit doesn't require superior intelligence or specialized skills. All it requires is the will to cultivate the habit of making things happen.

Obstacle No. 1: Resistance to Change

Homeostasis, the tendency to cling to the status quo, or existing conditions, and avoid change is a common human trait. Unfortunately, it is also a self-defeating and self-destructive habit. Of all the negative things that can be said about the phenomenon of homeostasis, the worst is that it defies the laws of nature. The reality is that life *is* change, from the generation and dying of cells in your body to the construction and demolition of buildings in a city. Weather changes; laws change; the economy changes; the reins of power change; technology changes; and, perhaps most significant of all, your age changes every second of your life.

I thought a lot about this problem at a young age, because I was acutely aware of my own resistance to change. I concluded that the heart of the problem was fear—fear of the unknown. We all grow comfortable with existing conditions, even those we dislike.

For sheer physical discomfort, the worst experience of my life was serving in the Army. I never had been away from home for any significant length of time prior to my unpleasant Army experience, yet the phenomenon of homeostasis took hold of me during my tour of duty. I was in the artillery, the one branch of the military where continual uprooting, moving, and digging in at new locations is a given. Constant state of change is a way of life in the artillery.

Artillery personnel are trained to treat each new position as a permanent home because their length of stay in any given location is always unknown. It could be as little as ten minutes or as long as ten weeks. What surprised me was that each time we pitched our tents and got settled, I mentally resisted uprooting again. I remember one stretch in particular when we stayed in the same area of snow-covered mountains for over a week in zero-degree weather. My tent became home to me, and I "set up house" as comfortably as possible. I'll never forget the mental twinge I felt when we were ordered to dismantle our tents, get our gear together, and move out. As miserable and cold as it was in those mountains, I had become accustomed to my little routine.

If something as inherently unpleasant as sleeping in a tent—in the mountains, in snow and cold, in the Army—can become comfortable to someone, it's easy to see why we become accustomed to situations in everyday life that are nowhere near as bleak. As a result, people get stuck in dead-end jobs, professions they dislike, and other conditions that make their lives miserable. What usually keeps them from taking life-changing action is fear of the unknown.

To overcome such fear, the first thing you must do is accept the reality that circumstances surrounding your life will change, regardless of whether or not you want them to. The only unknowns are how and when. It's up to you to decide whether you want to direct the changes, or whether you're content to react to them. The problem with the latter approach is that it leads to a lack of control, which almost always leads to negative results. Always remember: That which you can confront you can control; that which you cannot confront will control you.

Finally, it's a matter of how you frame the phenomenon of change in your mind. If you think of change as the essence of life—as an exciting, integral part of the living experience—you can wipe fear from your consciousness. Best of all, I've found this to be a relatively easy thing to accomplish, because experience has taught me that change *is* exciting. I never cease to be amazed when I look back on my life and see how many major changes have taken place in a relatively short period of time and how most of those changes have been for the better.

Put another way, if change is inevitable—and it is—why not assign it a positive rather than a negative value? By so doing, you'll find that it will be much easier for you to develop the Action Habit, and to be able to control much of the change that takes place as you strive toward the achievement of your objectives.

Obstacle No. 2: Waiting for Something to Happen
As mentioned earlier, many people naively assume that everyone else is vitally interested in their affairs. Unfortunately, it simply isn't so. In business, in particular, it's important to come to grips with the reality that no one cares about your deal as much as you do.

Perhaps you've noticed that if you have something the other party wants, your phone rings off the hook. But if you need cooperation from the other party to get a deal closed that's more important to you than him, you're lucky if he returns your calls. Talk about facing reality, like it or not, that's the way the real world works. It's also the reason that when you're on pins and needles and ready to close a deal, your investor mysteriously goes on vacation for two weeks without giving you advance notice, your accountant leaves for the day to play golf, and Legalman frantically searches his little black book to find someone to treat him to lunch (and, at the same time, allow Legalman to bill him for the honor).

The point is that the more you have on the line, the more it's up to you to take action—to make things happen—because no one else cares. It's always safest to assume that your deal is important only to you. When you fall into the lethargic habit of waiting for others to take action on your behalf, you're doomed to disappointment. **Real-World Rule No. 64: If you want something to happen, make it happen.**

In discussing the concept of value for value, I suggested that if you want more, you should make yourself worth more. However, I certainly didn't mean to imply that everyone with whom you deal will agree on what your reward should be. If you get results for people, that only puts you in a position to ask for more. In most cases, however, you still have to take the initiative and let people know what you think you're worth.

In other words, you shouldn't naively assume that others will see to it that you receive maximum remuneration. Even if the other party is value-for-value oriented, that doesn't mean he has omniscient powers to recognize your true value. While you have to be careful not to overvalue what you bring to the table, it's also up to you to make it a regular habit to ask for what you're worth. **Real-World Rule No. 134: All other things being equal, the mere act of asking can be the main difference between one person's success and another person's mediocre station in life.**

I first thought about this principle when a friend of mine (some of whose trials and tribulations I discussed in Chapter 2), who was an attorney specializing in securing cable-television franchises, told me about the evolution of his career. For years he was just a normal deal-killing attorney—drafting unintelligible legal documents and having three-martini lunches at the expense of his clients—until one day he decided to ask for what he thought he was worth. Until then, he had charged his clients an hourly rate, but he made up his mind he was going to up his income by charging not only for his time, but by also asking for a percentage of each deal.

Sure enough, he convinced the next client who walked through the door that it was in the client's best interest to give him a piece of his deal. It not only gave Legalman an incentive to get the results the client wanted, but to get them as quickly as possible. It's enough to take one's breath away to contemplate Legalman not having to spend the majority of his time trying to figure out how to kill his client's deal. Within a few years, Legalman ended up owning varying percentages of numerous cable-television stations and became very wealthy—all because he had the courage to ask for what he thought he was worth.

Real-World Rule No. 65: When you depend on no one but yourself, not only can you can never be disappointed, you also increase the chances of controlling your destiny. It's foolhardy to sit back and wait for things to happen. The wise person cultivates the habit of *making them happen.*

Obstacle No. 3: The Time Is Never Right

Talk about a procrastinator's dream, this is it—probably the most insidious of all obstacles to taking action. If you're waiting for everything to be just right before taking action, you are in possession of a foolproof excuse for failure. **Real-World Rule No. 111: Conditions are never right at the right time; the timing is always wrong.**

When people cling to the excuse that the time isn't right to do something, it's often because, as mentioned earlier, they are emotionalising the word *hard* and confusing it with the word *impossible.* It's not impossible to change occupations right now; just hard. It's not impossible to move to another city right now; just hard. It's not impossible to terminate a bad partnership right now; just hard. The tendency to see hard as impossible is closely tied to the natural tendency to resist change. Don't delude yourself into believing that just because something is difficult, it's impossible.

In addition to its close connection to the problem of resistance to change, confusing hard with impossible is often tied to a trait I discussed in association with good human relations: flexibility. It's important to understand that the opportunity available to you at any given time will never be the perfect opportunity. Life doesn't work that way. The inability to cope with the imperfections of life leads only to frustration and inaction.

While it's a healthy perspective to believe that the best deal in the world comes along every day, it's equally healthy to acknowledge that there's no such thing as a perfect deal. There are times when the deal that's available to you may just be the deal you need at that moment. I recall a friend of mine telling me that a year prior to his being named president of CBS Radio, he accepted a job as general manager of a CBS Radio affiliate station in Sacramento, California. When I asked him how in the world he had found himself in such an unglamorous situation just twelve months before landing the top spot at CBS Radio, he replied, "Let me just say that the job I took in Sacramento wasn't the deal I wanted, but, due to a variety of personal circumstances, it was the deal I *needed* at that particular time."

Above all, don't allow yourself to be lulled into the New Year's Resolution Syndrome, rationalizing away each wasted day by thinking, "I'm going to work on improving my efficiency starting the first of the year" or "I'm going to start making ten sales calls a day beginning next month" or "I'm going to start working on that project as soon as I get everything else under control." The New Year's Resolution Syndrome is a first cousin to The Exception. It's the antithesis of living in the present, and leads only to a life of endless procrastination.

The time to start becoming more efficient is today. The time to make a sales call is today. The time to start working on a project is today. The time to start picking up the pieces and begin over again is today. Develop the habit of living in the present. The best day really is today, so get started now, no matter what your problems are and no matter how long you've already procrastinated.

Obstacle No. 4: Self-Doubt
Self-doubt is a much more common problem than many people would like to believe. I am convinced that, to one extent or another, everyone—and I do mean everyone—harbors self-doubt. It's a trait we're handed with our birth certificate.

The average person has a bigger-than-life view of great athletes, show-business celebrities, and other public figures, and, as a result, has a difficult time picturing them as mere mortals. Nonetheless, having known many public figures through the years, I can testify that their generally inflated images are grossly inaccurate. Some of the most insecure people I've known are outrageously wealthy, very famous, or both.

Bob Cousy, the legendary Hall-of-Fame, ex-Boston Celtics guard, once said in an interview, ". . . even the great [athletes] choke at one point or another. The ones that deny it are liars. They're lying to themselves and they're lying to the public." These are surprising words, coming from a superstar from yesteryear noted for his clutch performances in the NBA. Arguably, the reason a great athlete chokes is that he, at least subconsciously, loses confidence; or, to put it in corollary terms, he gets a rush of self-doubt at the moment of truth.

Realizing that people we look up to also harbor self-doubt helps to put the matter in proper perspective. Just knowing you're not alone, that you're not some kind of freak because you sometimes experience a twinge of self-doubt, can serve as a good first step toward overcoming the problem.

A second aid in overcoming self-doubt is to ask yourself, "What are the downside consequences if I should fail to accomplish my objective?" It's important to remember that events rarely turn out to be anywhere near as bad as we picture them. Continually reminding yourself to analyze honestly and objectively what might be the worst-case consequences of a failure goes a long way toward reducing self-doubt. Objective analysis usually reveals that self-doubt is based more on emotion than reality.

Third, we live in a very negative world, a world where we continually meet people who try to convince us that what we want to do can't be done. In truth, every successful person in history has been told—many times—that what he wanted to accomplish couldn't be done. In an article about Fred Astaire the day after he died, I was amused by a quote from a critic's review early in Astaire's career: "Can't act. Can't sing. Balding. Can dance a little." Such is the story of life. The important question is whether or not a person allows this kind of negative input to prevent him from taking action.

Unfortunately, most people do allow the continual barrage of negative input from others to render them immobile. When people repeatedly bombard our heads with negative mental darts, it's very difficult to keep from thinking, "Maybe they're right. Maybe I can't do it." It's another one of those vicious cycles: The more you hear you can't accomplish something, the more self-doubt you have; and the more self-doubt you have, the easier target you are for those who thrive on bombarding others with negativism. Beware: This cycle can lead to failure if you don't make it a habit to short-circuit it as quickly as possible.

Finally, to overcome self-doubt you must face the reality that you *will* fail—often, and in a big way. This is where the Natural Law of Balance and the law of averages again come into play. No matter how long you wait, no matter how much you try to prepare yourself, you're still going to make mistakes. It's one of those inevitabilities of life, a reality of being human.

Knowing this, I've developed a trick that I play on my mind, one that conditions it to look at action as an opportunity to actually practice making mistakes. If you've read many biographies of famous people, you know that the path to greatness is always littered with mistakes and failures. I'm convinced that one way in which super-achievers become great is by learning through their mistakes. In the words of Richard Bach, "That's what learning is, after all: not whether we lose the game, but how we lose and how we've changed because of it, and what we take away from it that we never had before, to apply to other games. Losing, in a curious way, is winning."

I thought about the wisdom of Bach's words when a friend of mine, Marsh Fisher, told me the remarkable story of how he and his partner built Century 21 Real Estate into an international success. Through most of his life, Marsh was like millions of other would-be entrepreneurs, trying his hand at a number of occupations, but never quite finding his niche. He kicked around from one venture to another until, at age forty-four, he became involved in a franchise venture in the San Fernando Valley area of Los Angeles. However, after two years of tough going, the company failed.

Marsh then came up with a new franchising idea, one that he believed would lead to a megasuccess. He spent two years trying to find someone to back his idea, one that was based on what he had learned from the failure of the San Fernando Valley venture. Finally, at age forty-seven, he got someone to put up $6,000 to help get it off the ground. Within six months, Marsh Fisher's new company was able to sell about sixty franchises in Southern California, even though it had virtually no working capital, no experience, no existing franchises to display as models, and no fancy brochures or literature.

The most important lesson to learn from this story is that an idea, when coupled with action, can indeed be a very powerful force. But what I found most significant about Marsh Fisher's story is when he told me, "If I hadn't first tried and failed in the franchising venture in the San Fernando Valley, there's absolutely no way my partner and I could have made a success of Century 21. The things I learned the first time around were the key to Century 21's success."

The mistakes Marsh Fisher made in his first franchising venture were unpleasant, to be sure, but they were necessary to learn what he needed to know to win over the long term. This, I am convinced, is an important key to overcoming self-doubt. You must develop the habit of thinking of mistakes as opportunities to learn and grow. With that kind of perspective, it then becomes much easier to take action.

Obstacle No. 5: Adversity
In discussing self-doubt as an obstacle to action, I was referring primarily to the individual who is afraid to take the first step, who can never bring himself to leave the starting gate. Adversity,

however, is a different kind of obstacle. When I speak of adversity as an obstacle to action, I'm referring to the individual who has taken action—perhaps many times—but, due to obstacles, rejection, bad luck, and/or disappointment over lack of results, has become too discouraged to continue. Though I used Marsh Fisher's story to illustrate how viewing mistakes as learning opportunities can help a person overcome self-doubt, his story also is a classic example of overcoming adversity.

It's essential to be able to overcome adversity as an obstacle to taking action, because, without exception, there's no such thing as success without adversity. As I pointed out earlier, no matter how well things are going for you at any given time, fortune tires of carrying anyone on her shoulders too long. Problems are inevitable. Life often seems to be a perpetual attempt to fit square pegs into round holes.

The essential trait needed to overcome adversity is perseverance, most of the ingredients for which are to be found in the first nine chapters of this book. Perseverance requires knowledge and wisdom. In particular, it takes a clear understanding of the reality that problems are an integral, ongoing part of life . . . of the Natural Law of Balance . . . of the law of averages . . . and of the power of the mind to determine, to a great extent, one's destiny.

To the degree a person possesses an understanding of these realities, he demonstrates belief, which in turn leads to an expansive mental paradigm (which, for all practical purposes, is synonymous with having a positive mental attitude). Also, it's important to remember that an expansive mental paradigm represents a resourceful, or alternative-thinking, mind, a mind that continually searches for new solutions no matter what kind of roadblocks it is confronted with.

To be motivated to carry on in the face of adversity, an individual needs desire, which comes about as a result of correctly answering the Present Living Questions discussed in Chapter 4. The answers to these questions give meaning to a person's life, which in turn gives him the desire to keep going in spite of obstacles, opposition, discouragement, and bad luck. Adversity, then, tests your commitment to your goals. Plain and simple, the probability of success in any venture is increased in direct proportion to your willingness to keep going in spite of obstacles. If you want something badly enough, you won't give up; if not, you will.

It might be appropriate to say that an expansive mental paradigm and desire are the father and mother, respectively, of perseverance. Two other ingredients determine the *degree* of an individual's perseverance: time and focus. To persevere over the long term, you have to have the self-discipline to keep focused on your main objective and be patient until things finally come together for you.

Given what's involved, it's easy to understand why most people do not display a great deal of perseverance. That's unfortunate, considering that perseverance probably is the most powerful success tool known to man. Perseverance is the ultimate manifestation of the Action Habit, because it is continual action. Perseverance means being able to handle massive rejection, massive disappointment, and massive frustration. It's what makes you persist long after the other guy has given up. In fact, if you stop to think about it, no one can defeat you. Defeat can occur only when *you* decide to quit. And the nice thing about it is that there's no limit to the number of times you can try.

Perseverance is a trait so powerful that it can overcome almost any deficiency. It will always put you at an advantage over the individual with more brains or talent, because neither intelligence nor skill are involved. Personally, I've never tried to kid myself about my IQ or talents. There have been very few days in my life that I haven't met someone who is far smarter and/or far more talented than I am.

Whatever success I've managed to achieve, I attribute to my being perhaps the most relentless, resilient, perseverant individual I know. I practice simple success habits on a regular basis—success habits that are accessible to everyone—and so long as I maintain the self-discipline to keep focused, these habits never fail me. Admittedly, it's not as attention-getting as being gifted with special talents, but the idea is to play the hand you're dealt with as best you can. Remember, it's what you *do* with what you *have.*

As with the obstacle of feeling overwhelmed, over the years I've developed a systematic approach to handling adversity, steps that you, too, can easily implement whenever you feel as though obstacles are jamming your action gears.

Step Number One. Never take the attitude, "Well, at least things can't get any worse." Trust me, they can. While it's nice to be imperturbable, it's also unwise to be too cavalier when adversity strikes. It's important to move swiftly into action, particularly if the adversity has disastrous implications.

Step Number Two. Call time-out and mentally and physically come to a complete stop. Panic is an irrational, quick-spreading fear. If you're irrational, your perception of reality is warped. As a result, panic tends to promote short-term relief at the expense of long-term success.

Step Number Three. Stop the hemorrhaging. This means minimizing the damage, which you do by stabilizing the situation as quickly as possible. In financial terms, it means avoid throwing good money after bad.

Step Number Four. Stand back and get a big-picture perspective of the battlefield. Is this really a life-or-death matter? Are you, or is anyone in your family, terminally ill or in physical danger? And even if it is a genuine disaster, is it possible to pick up the pieces and start over again?

Step Number Five. In a rigidly self-disciplined manner, focus exclusively on the crux of the problem. To do this, you have to eliminate all excess baggage. Simply refuse to make exceptions for anyone or anything. Firmly stick to your guns, and have the courage to say *no* to everyone. If someone tries to get you to take your eye off the ball—like trying to coax you into watching Monday Night Football—just look him in the eye and calmly say, "Sorry, I'd love to, but I'm being executed in the morning."

Step Number Six. Carefully and honestly analyze the problem in terms of what *you* did wrong. It's essential that you not focus on what others did. In other words, avoid the delusion of transference. To the extent you blame others, you only succeed in evading the real issue and thereby make it virtually impossible to figure out what you have to do, not only to solve the problem at hand, but to see that it never happens again.

Also, to a responsible person, there's no such thing as mitigating circumstances. A so-called mitigating circumstance is really just a reason why something happened to you, but it doesn't excuse you from the fact you allowed it to happen. Develop the habit of figuring out what *you* did wrong, so you can get on with doing something about it.

Step Number Seven. Start moving in the right direction as quickly as possible. Concentrate on maximizing the positives of the situation and implementing long-term, permanent solutions in order to avoid setting up still more balloon notes for yourself down the road. Forget about the adversity you've just experienced—let go of it completely—and get on with your life. This may involve making major changes, because extreme problems often call for extreme solutions.

As you can see, applying the Action Habit to the problem of adversity is a mental task that requires hard work. It's difficult to accept that there's only one way to handle a crisis effectively, and that's to meet it head on. You learn to solve problems by dealing with them, not by running away.

Finally, it's helpful to view adversity in proper perspective. As unpleasant as adversities are, they're really just opportunities to grow, and personal growth leads to long-term success. Thus, failure acts as a process-of-elimination device in that each failure brings you one step closer to success. You can't afford to let up, because you never know when you might be just one step away from victory. As you've seen throughout this book, the practice of alternative-thinking and the Natural Law of Balance make adversity little more than future success masquerading as failure. In addition, the Natural Law of Balance assures us that the longer we work to achieve something, the more meaningful it becomes.

The Greatest of All Dangers

The most important lesson to be learned from this chapter is that taking no action is the greatest danger of all. Remember, even inaction is a form of action—passive action—and therefore has consequences. The problem is that you don't control those consequences, because they're consequences by default. In other words, if you don't take the initiative, events will control you. That, in turn, means that you will be *reacting* instead of *acting*.

An old maxim says that "you have to take a chance to get a chance," so no matter how successful you may be in cultivating the nine other major success habits I've discussed in previous chapters, it's all for naught if you don't take action. The Action Habit literally is a life-or-death matter. Life is action; death is inaction. You'll have plenty of time for the latter at some (hopefully) far off time in the future.

The Choice Is Yours

I again emphasize that there is no big secret to success, that achieving positive results has little to do with superior intelligence or special skills of any kind, and that formal education, hard work, and luck are incidental to an individual's place on the success ladder. Chances are that you're already a lot closer to getting where you want to be in life than you realize. Remember, the difference between stupendous success and colossal failure is remarkably small.

The choice is yours: You can spend your time hoping to find the mysterious secret to success that eludes the average person throughout life, or you can put your efforts into cultivating the same sound, simple habits that all successful people routinely practice. I personally can guarantee you that the latter is the most certain way to win big over the long term. One last time: Success is not a grand-slam home run.

As I stated in the Introduction, two realities make Million Dollar Habits a very exciting proposition: First, they work. Second, they can be learned by anyone who is willing to put forth the necessary effort. The operative word here is *effort*. While these habits are simple enough to learn, to practice them requires serious, constant effort.

Is there another alternative? Yes. If practicing Million Dollar Habits sounds like too much work, you always have the option of choosing to live a completely tranquil life. After all, tranquility is just a lobotomy away.

Robert Ringer is an American icon whose insights into life have helped more people transform their aspirations and goals into reality than perhaps any other author in history. For more than three decades, his works have stood alone as the gospel when it comes to conveying worldly wisdom to millions of readers worldwide.

He is the author of two *New York Times* #1 bestsellers, both of which have been listed by the *New York Times* among the 15 bestselling motivational books of all time. He is also the publisher of RobertRinger.com, where he combines philosophy, reality, and action in his trademark style that translates into tangible results for his readers.

Ringer has appeared on numerous national television and radio shows, including *The Tonight Show, Today, The Dennis Miller Show, Good Morning America, ABC Nightline, The Charlie Rose Show,* and has made a variety of appearances on Fox News and Fox Business.

He has also been the subject of feature articles in such major publications as *Time, People,* the *Wall Street Journal, Fortune, Barron's,* and the *New York Times.*

To learn about Robert Ringer's life-changing new program, *Fast Track to Dealmaking Fortunes,* visit http://robertringer.com/mdh.